SIGNED BY

BAXTER

MOMENTS
WITH
BAXTER

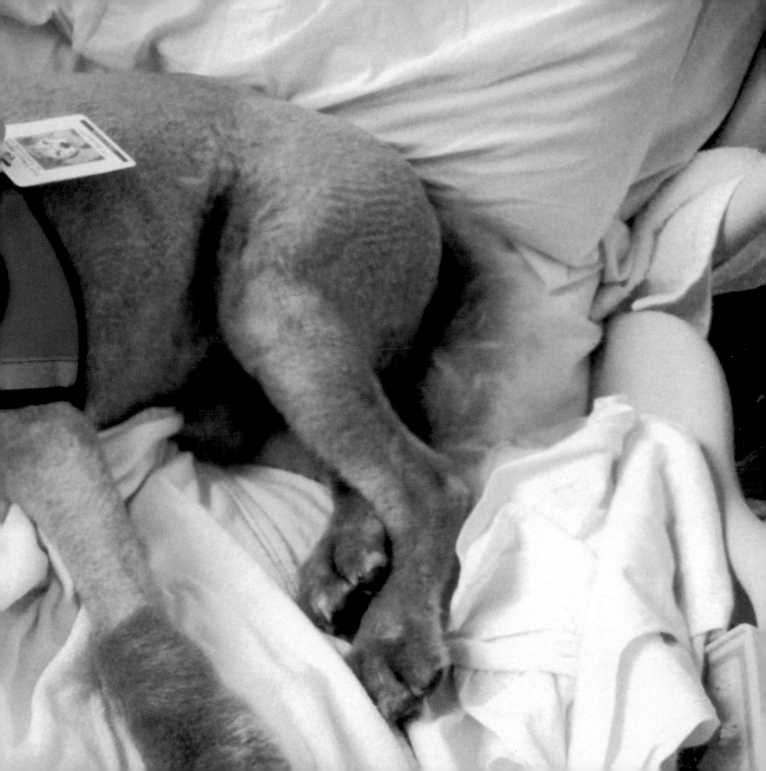

"You're in the arms of an Angel;
may you find some comfort here"

— FROM "ANGEL"
BY SARAH McLACHLAN

SAGE
PRESS
San Diego, California

MOMENTS
— WITH —
BAXTER

MELISSA JOSEPH

Photographs by Dennis Bussey

"Therapy Dog Training"
by J. Alieta Downer, Cape-Able Canines

CONTENTS

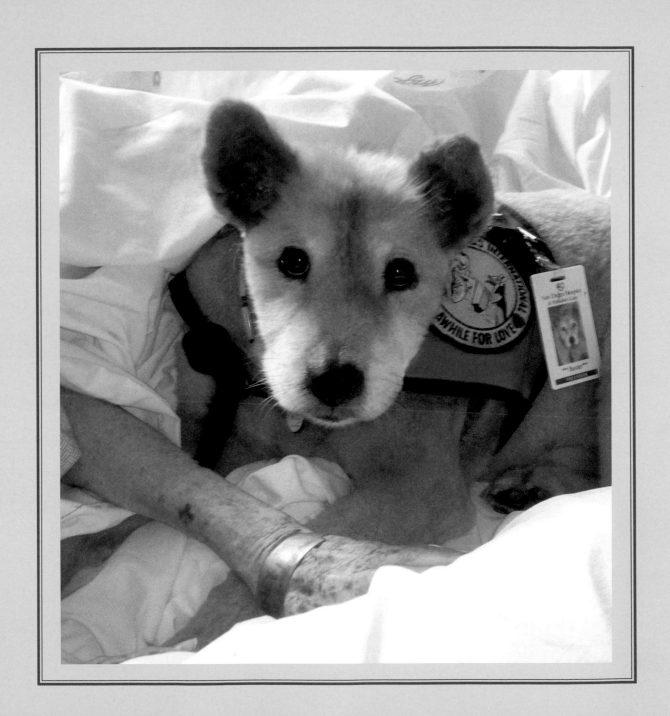

— INTRODUCTION —

Baxter is a rescue dog. He's part golden retriever and part chow; he's a golden chow. We often refer to him as a "love" breed. He's now eighteen years old and afflicted with many problems, from pancreatitis to high blood pressure to a thyroid condition to acute arthritis and chronic bronchitis, which give him his signature limp and cough, respectively. As a result, he's great for therapy work, because patients can identify with him.

I got Baxter when he was about two years old. He was going to be euthanized because he had heartworms and his owners could not afford to treat him. A friend of mine saved Baxter but could not keep him herself, as she already had too many dogs she had rescued. She called me and described him as adorable, adding, "Will you take him, please?"

It took about six weeks for me to make friends with Baxter. It was obvious that something had happened to him, that he had been abused in some way.

He cowered whenever I had something large in my hand and became very fearful when he heard any loud noise, such as a bouncing ball or a book hitting the floor.

I loved Baxter for many, many years, never knowing that I was grooming and training him to become the world's best therapy dog. I took him everywhere with me; he was very well socialized. He slept with me, grew up with my cat, and was completely loved by all who met him. I even opened a doggie store because of Baxter. Though it wasn't successful, Baxter learned about going to work, greeting customers, and interacting with other dogs. When we closed the store, I had an auction and donated all the proceeds to the local animal rescue league in Jackson, Mississippi.

After that, Baxter and I moved to San Diego, where he found his *raison d'être*. Perhaps the same thing happened to me. When my husband, Dennis, and I went through the volunteer orientation program at San Diego Hospice and The Institute for Palliative Medicine, Baxter attended the three all-day Saturday sessions with us. There, the volunteer coordinators fell in love with him and were amazed at how well he socialized with the more than thirty participants in the program. In fact, on the final Saturday, when all the participants received certificates of completion, everyone stood and clapped when he walked up to receive his certificate. This was the first step toward his life's calling.

One of the orientation organizers gave us the name of Therapy Dogs International, one of the companies that officially certifies dogs for therapy. We immediately investigated and several months later, after Baxter had aced the rigorous test, the three of us began volunteering at the In-Patient Care Facility at San Diego Hospice, a 24-room facility where patients go when death is imminent. Everyone at In-Care knows Baxter, from the janitor to the CARE ambulance service that transports the patients. All these people know him as a real hero, the Angel of Hospice.

As you read these stories, you will witness the magical connection between patient and canine. We hope that you will be inspired to train your own dog to be a therapy dog. We hope that you will be motivated to become a volunteer at hospice or at another hospital or facility. We hope for these things because these experiences have been the most rewarding of our lives, as well as being rewarding for those with whom we share them.

Volunteering at hospice has the added benefit of demystifying this phenomenon known as death. Yes, death is sad, but you will learn that it does not have to be feared. San Diego Hospice and The Institute for Palliative Medicine and all hospices have a wonderful, reassuring motto that we love: "No one should die alone; no one should die in pain." We, along with all the others who work there, do whatever we can to ensure that quality of life continues until the very last breath.

ALL PROCEEDS FROM THE SALE OF THIS BOOK
WILL GO TO CHARITABLE CAUSES
SUCH AS SAN DIEGO HOSPICE AND
THE INSTITUTE FOR PALLIATIVE MEDICINE,
THERAPY DOGS INTERNATIONAL,
ANIMAL SHELTERS, AND OTHERS.

HOW BAXTER
BECAME ——
A THERAPY DOG

One day, about four years ago, my husband, Dennis, came home with a suggestion. "Sweetie, we're going to volunteer at San Diego Hospice. I just met a couple who volunteer there and I'm convinced this would be a good experience for us. I have the proper paperwork right here. We can fill it out and send it in and get started."

Because I was interested in doing something more than teaching English and composition at a local community college, I agreed to explore this as a possible way to make a difference.

I was skeptical, though not of working at hospice. I'm one of those people who is not afraid to embrace the mystery of the dark side of life, and I seem to have a gift for bringing compassion and humor to it. My reticence was about the mandatory attendance at the orientation program, which demanded that I give up three Saturdays and attend a workshop at hospice.

In addition, I never like to leave Baxter home alone for long periods of time. Even at this time he was getting old, and I was trying to keep him as vital as possible. Then I found out that the gorgeous hospice facility where the workshop would take place is dog friendly, so of course I decided to bring Baxter.

For many years, Baxter has accompanied me almost everywhere I go. He is the most well-behaved, socialized, and compliant dog I have ever met. He never whines and rarely barks; he doesn't even nudge me for attention. He introduces himself to those he senses are receptive to him, and ignores those who are not. He forms a unique relationship with every person he meets. He has never been formally trained and knows no commands, but he is always quiet, resilient, and obedient.

As he usually does, Baxter charmed each of the over thirty participants at the orientation, including the staff who presided over the meetings. When he was not in someone else's lap, he waited patiently beside me on his mat. Toward the end of the orientation, when we were being photographed for our identification badges, one of the staff members suggested that Baxter be photographed for his ID as well. "You know, he is an incredibly special dog. You might want to look into getting him certified."

"Certified, what do you mean by that?"

"Well, there's this organization, Therapy Dogs International (TDI), where you can find out how to get Baxter trained and certified as a therapy dog. I believe he would be a wonderful volunteer here in the In-Patient Care Center."

I was intrigued.

After the meeting, a veteran volunteer approached me. He had participated in a panel of well-seasoned volunteers both in homes and at the in-patient facility. He seemed to have found himself through giving at hospice. He, too, encouraged me to get Baxter certified. "There's just something special about your dog. I am drawn to his calmness."

"I appreciate what you're saying. I do plan on following through in doing what it takes to certify him."

As a grand finale to the orientation, each participant was presented with a certificate of completion, authorizing us to begin our volunteering. The last name approved was Baxter's. Even though he had to get certified before he could volunteer, the organizers recognized his wonderful contribution to the group.

I was already getting excited, even though I had no clue what getting Baxter certified entailed. The next day I contacted TDI and began the process. I requested the appropriate packet, took Baxter to my local veterinarian for a complete physical, and made an appointment with the certification officer in my district.

A couple of weeks later, Dennis, Baxter, and I arrived at the certification officer's home for the test. If I had read the test questions in advance, I would have sworn to you that Baxter would never pass. Dennis, Baxter, and I arrived completely ignorant about what was required. Most dogs are trained to become therapy dogs. Most dogs rehearse the test questions before the actual test is administered. Not Baxter. His parents brought him to his test unprepared, unrehearsed, and unpolished.

How could I be so stupid?

I got Baxter out of the car and we made our introductions. The officer made a comment that eased my anxiety just a little. "This is perhaps the cutest dog I've ever tested."

"Well, he may be the cutest, but he's also the least trained."

The test is very difficult. Baxter should have failed at the first question, but on this day he was accompanied by an angel. He got all the responses right, though I truly don't know how he managed to do that.

Here are the questions and commands to which Baxter responded with grace and confidence:

- "Sit, Baxter." This seems like a basic command, but I never make Baxter sit on the concrete. I always provide a soft surface. I didn't know what Baxter would do. He sat, but I felt like we barely made it through question one.

- "Stay, Baxter."

- I was instructed to walk away 150 feet and call to my dog. "Come here, Baxter." He came.

- He had to walk and heel.

- The certification officer brought in another dog, and Baxter had to ignore him. Baxter remained aloof and stayed by my side. I was amazed.

- Next, the officer brought out a bowl of food. Baxter was not permitted to go near the food. I mimicked a command I've heard in the past: "Leave it." Ha, it worked! Baxter was still by my side.

- Then, the officer had someone in a wheelchair try to run over Baxter. "You've got to be kidding," I mumbled to myself as I glared at Dennis. My eyes told him, "This is it. Baxter will never make the cut." He seemed to understand what I was saying and nodded his head in agreement. To both our surprise, Baxter didn't react. He was calm, stable, and stationary.

- Next, the officer threw commercial-size stainless steel bowls on the concrete. Baxter could not flinch, cringe, or run. He remained motionless. I mouthed to Dennis, "Go figure."

- Then, someone tried to run over Baxter with an electric scooter. Again, Baxter did not react. It was as if he were meant to do this.

- Next, someone took a cane and whipped it all around Baxter. Since Baxter is a rescue dog who typically flinches when anyone is holding an implement or when he hears a loud noise, I have always assumed that someone once hurt him. He did not flinch today. I was really impressed now.

- Someone wailed and flailed. No response from Baxter.

- Nancy grabbed his tail, pulled his ears, smothered his face with her hands. Baxter was still, with no reaction. Perfect.

- All this wasn't enough, however. Next she took her body and practically lay down on top of him. Surprisingly, he seemed to like it.

- "You both must leave Baxter with me now. I need to see if he has separation anxiety."

We walked away and stayed out of Baxter's sight for about twenty minutes. When we returned, Nancy had her arms around him.

"Did he pass?"

"He's going to be one wonderful therapy dog."

As soon as she said this, I began to cry and I hugged Dennis. He, too, was tearful. I hugged Baxter and said with an enthusiasm that he could understand, "You did it, Baxter. You did it. How did you know what to do? How did you understand those commands? I'm so proud of you!"

I will never understand how an untrained dog could act so perfectly, instinctively anticipating how he should react and taking his place in each of those unfamiliar, challenging situations. I can only imagine that it was because therapy work is something he was meant to do.

DENNIS BUSSEY

This is my husband, Dennis. Without him, this book would not have been possible. It was Dennis's idea that we start to volunteer at Hospice. Like Baxter, he helped to create each "moment" in the book. Then he captured each one with his digital camera.

Dennis approaches all his varied interests with unique vigor and passion. Whether it's growing tomatoes in our backyard, debating global warming, or volunteering with Baxter and me, he will impress you with his compassion, discipline, and integrity. He's the most stand-up man I know.

The pawprint seen throughout this book is made from an actual impression of Baxter's paw.

MELISSA JOSEPH

When I'm at hospice volunteering, I'm like Baxter. I'm in the moment. Nothing else matters. And I'm enriched by the experiences I have because of that. I think that death, seeing death, seeing pain, puts life into perspective. It gives me the knowledge that all we have is right now and it's essential to take that now and make it into something valuable. It's all about moments. And death is one of those moments.

Baxter never thinks about death. He only knows the moment. Because of that, with each exchange he has with a patient, family member, or friend, Baxter is giving 100 percent of his energy; and in return the love he receives nourishes his soul. At over eighteen, Baxter inhales and exhales love, moment by moment.

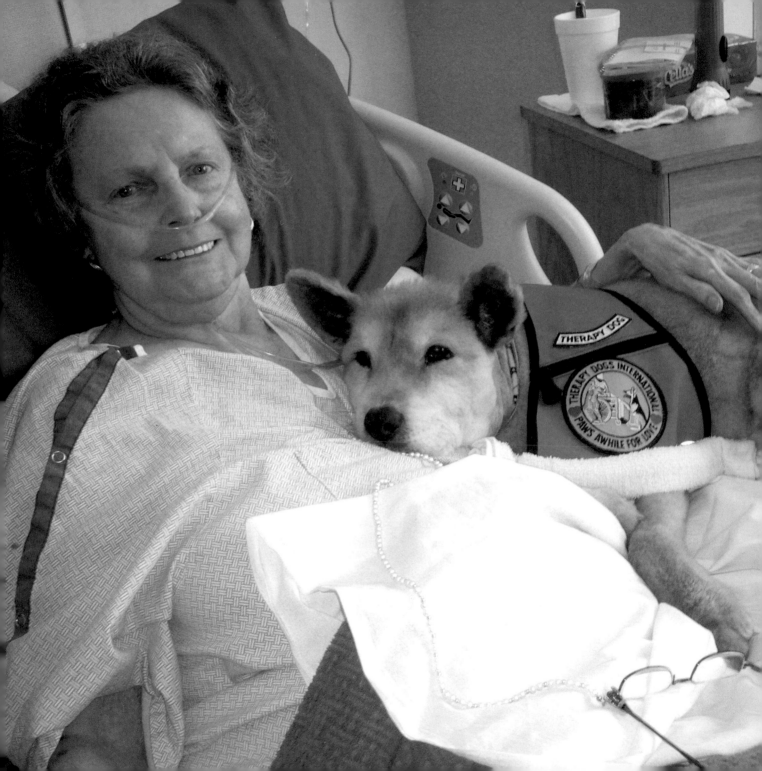

LIMIT STAY
— TO —
15 MINUTES

"Limit Stay to 15 Minutes." The sign is taped to Mo's door. I imagine that a nurse wheeled her to the art therapy table and helped her write this command on blue construction paper. Since Baxter knows no time limits on his love for a patient, I am sure that he will not be intimidated by her sign.

Cherry, one of the nurses, approaches Baxter and me. Her attention is completely directed to Baxter. "You're in great demand today. Mo is requesting to see you. She has already made a place for you in her bed. She's moved over to give you enough space to cuddle with her."

Baxter and I head toward the door with the sign.

"Hello, Mo."

"I've been waiting for Baxter. See, I have a place all laid out for him. I've moved over, and I think he can be right here." She points this out in a direct way by using both her eyes and her finger.

Baxter tries to fulfill her wishes, but she's not satisfied with his position. "I want him to be looking straight into my eyes."

"We've never had anyone choreograph Baxter's position." Dennis laughs as he says this.

Mo's head is resting on the king-size pillow she brought from home. With her own flowered pillowcase, the room has a homier feel. She's got this life-death connection all mapped out. Time with Baxter is like a get-together with one of her friends. He is the highlight of her day, the center of her room.

"What do you think about the temperature of the room?" she asks Baxter. "Would you like it cooler? I know you dogs like it really cool."

I proceed to turn down the thermostat. Anything for Mo, anything for Baxter. We all do this for our friends.

I put a pillow beside Mo as she instructs, and at last she's not fidgeting with Baxter's position. The whole process, though, is like an event. A friend named Baxter

I TAKE EACH
SOUND AND LOOK THAT
BAXTER GIVES MO
AND IT ALL
TRANSFERS TO A LOVE
THAT ENLARGES
MY HEART.

is coming over and she must get everything as she wants it. The arrangement is personal and the relationship is valuable. The sensitivity of being together is enhanced because death is so near. Much as with doing a hallucinogenic drug, each moment is highlighted and the words are bigger, more real, and more alive. I take each sound and look that Baxter gives Mo and it all transfers to a love that enlarges my heart.

Mo speaks to all three of us as if we've know her for years. Baxter keeps moving a little closer on his own accord. It's another day in Mo's life, even though she knows her death is imminent. Baxter is the inspiration. All moments are precious and worth living, even the last one.

"So, Mo, what's the deal with the sign on the door?"

"People, some people—well, not many people—some people who visit, just a few now and again, well, I don't want to outright lie, so I have the sign on the door for those who agitate, aggravate, or irritate, any of those "-ate" words will do. I don't want to have to tell them, so the sign does it for me."

We all laugh.

"I'm sure glad you guys have a sense of humor like I do. The doctor says that I have a great attitude and am witty. I'm hoping to piggyback on these two characteristics so that I can live at least until the eleventh. This is the day the new Harry

Potter book comes out. I've read them all. I'm so excited about this new one! I've prepaid for it with my green discount card and it's waiting for me at Borders. My niece will pick it up. I've already called over there to reconfirm they are holding it for me since I'm now at hospice and am dying. I told this to the salesman. I called him the other day to let him know where I was and that I was anticipating it. He said, 'Yes, Mrs. Thorne, I remember you. We'll have the book right here with your name on it.'

"You know I'm going to have to change that sign when I get the book: 'DO NOT ENTER, READING.' I'll be busy every day until I finish the book. I can't wait.

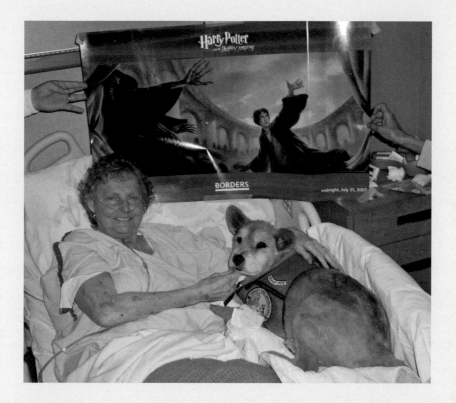

You know it's a heavy book and I can't hold it on my chest because of my pain there, so I've got my niece bringing me my little table with shiny legs that fold. That way I can read it comfortably here in bed.

"What I really want to do is see the movie before I die. It's not about the new book, but about one I've already read. I've seen them all, read them all. I hope I'm still alive to see that movie, but I don't know if hospice will allow me to go, and how I will be able to maneuver myself to get into the stadium seating."

"I have an idea," I say. "I am sure that we can make arrangements with both hospice and the manager of the theater to allow both you and Baxter to view the movie. Dennis and I can manage you and your wheelchair, and the nurses can make you a pain package for your journey."

"Too much liability," Mo says.

Dennis laughs. "It's about livability . . ."

"I like that word." Mo smiles.

Mo responds with tears in her eyes. She's ecstatic. She grabs on to Baxter with a newfound energy. "Oh, if get to go to that movie, I will have died and gone to heaven. Well, I won't be dead yet, will I?"

"Do you think you'll be able to sleep tonight?"

"Oh, yes, knowing that all this is possible. I know you have to go, but I must tell you one story before you leave. My husband, Jack, was very romantic. We had a very good marriage, almost thirty years, twenty-seven to be exact."

A wetness glosses over her small blue eyes but doesn't fall to her chalky face.

"When we met, I allowed him to give me a kiss. Well, I kissed him back, so that makes two. You can't go further than that at this point. Time went by, and we really loved each other.

"Jack was here at San Diego Hospice when he died five years ago. He had this idea that I take his ashes and spread some of them where we first kissed. Eighteen of my friends did this with me. Now, I have this idea to do the same with my ashes and I've planned for that. My niece, Kathy, will be in charge of this. Isn't that romantic? This is all the truth."

"Mo, I know you're telling us the truth. It's in your eyes."

This is something you cannot deny. Just like looking into Baxter's eyes. All that he is rests there: love, fear, and pain.

MO DID READ THE NEW HARRY POTTER BOOK.
AND SHE DID MAKE IT TO THE MOVIE, WITH BAXTER AS HER DATE.
SHE REMAINED IN HER WHEELCHAIR, AND BAXTER WAS BESIDE HER
IN HIS LITTLE RED PADDED WAGON. AS MO ATE POPCORN,
BAXTER WATCHED HER, KNOWING HER DREAM HAD COME TRUE.

SUPERMAN

—— IN A ——

SUPER BOY

Baxter is with Davide on several occasions. Dennis and I have no conversations with him other than his nodding "yes" to indicate he wants Baxter in bed with him. He connects with Baxter like a child connects to his teddy bear. Baxter becomes his link to the childhood that has slipped away as he confronts his death. At the same time, Baxter takes him to a place where death is not feared.

Davide's mother, Monica, is always there. Though she is the mother of several children, for these moments Davide is her only child. I struggle to reach her with words, for words can't penetrate the depth of her sadness. Only Baxter can bring her to a place of calm. She wraps herself in Davide's smile

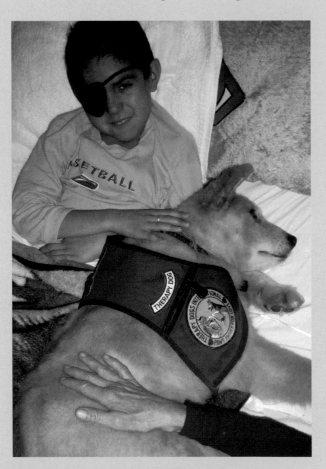

as Baxter and Davide silently relate. For these moments, all seems normal. As Baxter performs his magic, he becomes the conversation. He's the essential ingredient that transforms awkward moments into special, memorable ones. We have no reason to know more about this situation than what Baxter allows us to experience. Davide's face communicates it all.

I hug Monica when we arrive and again when we leave. All we can do is be there, and more important, bring Baxter for her dying six-year-old child.

On one occasion, while Baxter and Davide share a moment, one of Davide's doctors enters. Her mouth opens, but no words come out. She seems relieved to see Baxter in the arms of Davide.

"Maybe we should leave now and let you visit with Davide," I say.

"No, I think it's wonderful that Baxter is with Davide."

Baxter trumps her professional services at this stage in Davide's life . . . at this stage in his death.

As Baxter and Davide lie together, arm in arm on his Superman sheets, those of us watching hear words in the silence, though neither Baxter nor Davide can speak. Their hugs and stares have a singular definition: LOVE.

The only reason this moment isn't hopeless for Dennis and me is that Baxter provides a quality of life for Davide. With Davide, Dennis and I are truly helpless. It is all up to Baxter to bring joy. And for these moments, that's exactly what he does.

Davide appears very mature for his brief time on the planet. He has endured operations, much pain, and years of suffering, transforming him into a young man in a child's body. He is as courageous as Superman, his fighting spirit clearly visible.

This is a stage in Davide's life when moments with an old, suffering dog provide unspeakable identification. Baxter is closer to where Davide is going than any of us. We may never fully comprehend this until we are where Davide and Baxter are in life's journey.

Baxter is just what the doctor ordered.

> THIS IS A STAGE IN DAVIDE'S LIFE WHEN MOMENTS WITH AN OLD, SUFFERING DOG PROVIDE UNSPEAKABLE IDENTIFICATION. BAXTER IS CLOSER TO WHERE DAVIDE IS GOING THAN ANY OF US.

T H E L M A
— A N D   T H E —
R E D   H A T

Baxter and I approach Thelma, where she is outside in her wheelchair. Each of her sisters is at her side. Thelma, with shallow breaths, inhales the scent of the lovely flowers, perhaps for the last time. Even though it is short-sleeve weather, she wears a bright red knitted cap with a bill.

Her husband, with the expression of a pallbearer, ambles slowly toward his wife. His eyes are focused on the ground, his demeanor the antithesis of Thelma's. Her head is high and a smile adorns her tiny face, her spirit soaring in her liberating acceptance of her truncated life.

> BAXTER AND I WATCH
> HER BECOME
> MORE DISTANT UNTIL
> SHE COMPLETELY
> DISAPPEARS.

Later, inside hospice, Baxter and I again see Thelma, now shuffling alone, a sweater draped over one shoulder, still wearing her red hat. For the first time, she is in a hospice gown, with little turquoise socks and white sandals.

She comes out to greet me, but also to tell me that she is very busy with her family and cannot visit. She attempts to stoop over to reach out to Baxter, but her body stops short of touching him.

"I can't make it that far."

"Would you like for me to pick up Baxter so that you can pet him?"

"Yes, please."

I gather Baxter from the floor.

"Come on, Baxie, let's go see Thelma."

She reaches over to Baxter as I struggle to get him to just the right height for her.

"I am floating. I'm in no pain at all. Soon, though, I will die, but I'm okay. I love you, Baxter."

She takes off her hat and places it on Baxter's head. He understands this is a playful gesture of love and innocence, and raises his head, his mouth slightly open. Baxter doesn't try to shake off the hat; instead, he poses for Thelma and makes her laugh.

"I must go now."

"Good-bye, Thelma."

I rub her arm and kiss her cheek. I know this is the last time she will touch Baxter. She strolls back to her room the same way she strolled out.

Though her back is turned to me, I know she's smiling. Baxter and I watch her become more distant until she completely disappears . . .

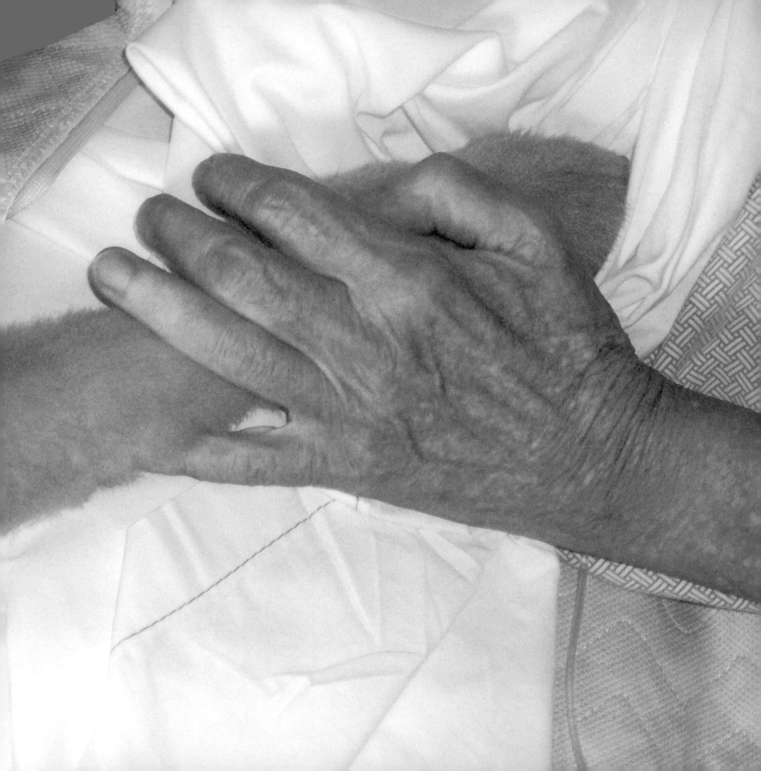

BAXTER

IS

INTUITIVE

A Hispanic family congregates outside the patient's room. Though they don't speak English, we can understand their tears and turned-down faces. As the three of us walk by the collection of embracing friends and family, from tots to adults, Baxter stops and looks up at the small needy crowd.

BAXTER STAYS RIGHT THERE FOR THESE MOMENTS IN WHICH HE ENABLES EACH OF THEM TO FEEL SOMETHING ELSE BESIDES THEIR PAIN. HE INDULGES THEM IN HIS WARMTH AND LOVE.

Baxter does not follow us to the nurses' station where we, with the help of the knowledgeable staff, discover which patient is a good match for him. We turn around and choose not to call him. We revel in his intuition to get right in the middle of these grieving people.

He sits down, and his body grazes a woman's foot. She reaches down to say hello and offers him a pat. This is just what he wants—their attention. That one touch has a domino effect. One person bends down to read his name tag, and another reaches out to examine the karma beads around his neck. A child sits on the floor next to him and makes noises that children make. Finally, the whole family begins petting him, and he responds by lying down while they continue to

SEP. 9 SUNDAY | AALL CARE
AIDE - BING
NURSE - KAREN
CNA - APRIL
Therapy DOG - BAXTER

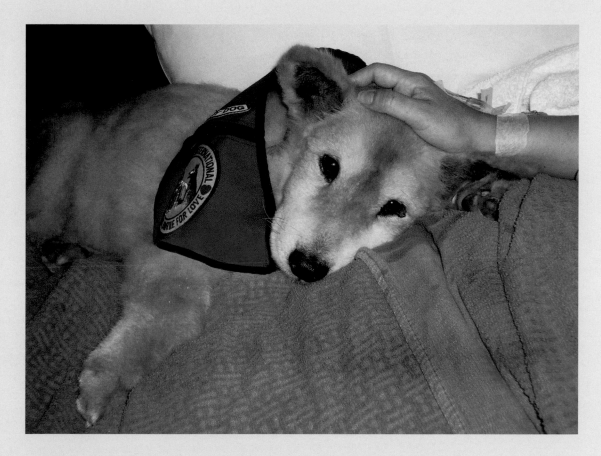

form a circle around him rather than around their mutual pain. It is as if he is the campfire bringing them warmth and light, offering some sort of sustenance for their sad hearts.

About twenty minutes pass, with people coming and going and Baxter staying . . . staying right there for these moments in which he enables each of them to feel something else besides their pain. He indulges them in his warmth and love.

IT'S THE
— LITTLE —
THINGS

I am walking Baxter around the grounds of hospice when an unfamiliar doctor approaches.

"What is this dog?" he says. "He's so cute! What kind is he?"

"This is Baxter," I reply, "and he gets in the bed with the patients here and makes everything better.

MARGUERITE'S VOICE BECOMES AMAZINGLY ANIMATED. HER EYES TWINKLE. THE FROWN HAS BEEN COVERED BY A SMILE.

He's just a wonderful little guy. Oh, he doesn't need to smell your hand first. You can just pet him."

"He's so soft. Wow! Now, tell me again what he does."

"Well, why don't you come with us to a room? We're on our way to see Marguerite."

Baxter leads the way.

"Hello, Marguerite. How would you like Baxter next to you?"

"Well, I don't know. I'm not sure today."

I can't believe she doesn't want Baxter by her side. This just isn't like her. I try another tactic.

"We brought you a present."

"You did?"

"Yeah, that funky headband we promised you. Remember?"

"Oh, I'm so glad! I've been in tears all morning about my hair falling out. I thought about cutting it all off. I really am conflicted and sad about it. Look at this."

She weaves her fingers through clumps of her short brunette hair.

"Check this out," I say. "This matches your eyes. You turn it inside out and start folding it and, *voilà*, you have a funky scarf to put around your head. See, Baxter has one around his neck. I pull it up over his head when it's cold.

"We brought you two of them, both with that turquoise color of your eyes. Let me demonstrate on myself and then you can see all the ways you can play with this thing."

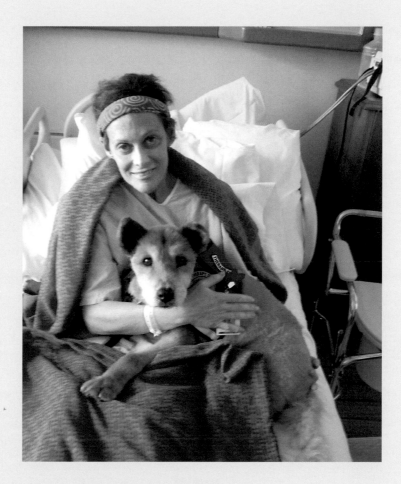

"Wow, that looks really cool. I love it!"

Marguerite's voice becomes amazingly animated. Her eyes twinkle. The frown has been covered by a smile. You would never know she is dying. This one gesture helps her feel more comfortable with her presence and therefore her state of being. It is so simple, yet so profound. The colorful scarf saves the day.

"Now, may I put it on you?" I ask.

"My head's really big."

I start putting it around her head. "Do you have a hand mirror?"

"Yes, right here," answers her aide. She gets up to adjust the handy-dandy mirror that comes with the tray table.

"No, that's too close," says Marguerite. "Move it back some. There. Wow, this looks fantastic!"

And it really does. The turquoise in the scarf is like matching eye shadow.

"Oh, I love it. It solves the problem."

She grins really big, snaps her fingers, and sings the words to a sixties tune as her head goes from left to right.

The doldrums have turned to moments of euphoria. I decide to pick up Baxter and put him beside her, without really asking. It seems like a good time now.

She reaches for him. "How's my Baxie boy? How's my baby dog?"

"Would you like him on your lap?"

"Yes."

She breathes sounds in Baxter's ear, and his ears stand up. Only Baxter knows what she is saying.

For the moment, it is easy to forget that Marguerite is dying. She's fitted with a new look and smitten with Baxter.

She turns to the observing doctor, who has yet to introduce himself. He's been standing at the edge of her room, unannounced and silent, with his eyes and mouth wide open. He shakes his head "no," which really means "yes." Yes, this moment is unbelievable.

I search within myself to hold back my tears. Goose bumps bubble up on my arms.

Marguerite turns to the doctor. "Do you need something from me?"

"No, I'm just here learning about what a therapy dog actually does for a patient. I've never seen this before and I need to understand the palliative effect of Baxter."

Marguerite does not reply. Instead she rocks Baxter.

Her cell phone rings and and her aide reaches for it for her.

"That's okay," Marguerite says. "I've got it. Oh, Kathy, hello. It's so good to hear from you."

In listening to that brief bit of conversation, you would think the two were going to talk about that latest movie they saw.

I remove Baxter from Marguerite's arms, and say good-bye with my eyes.

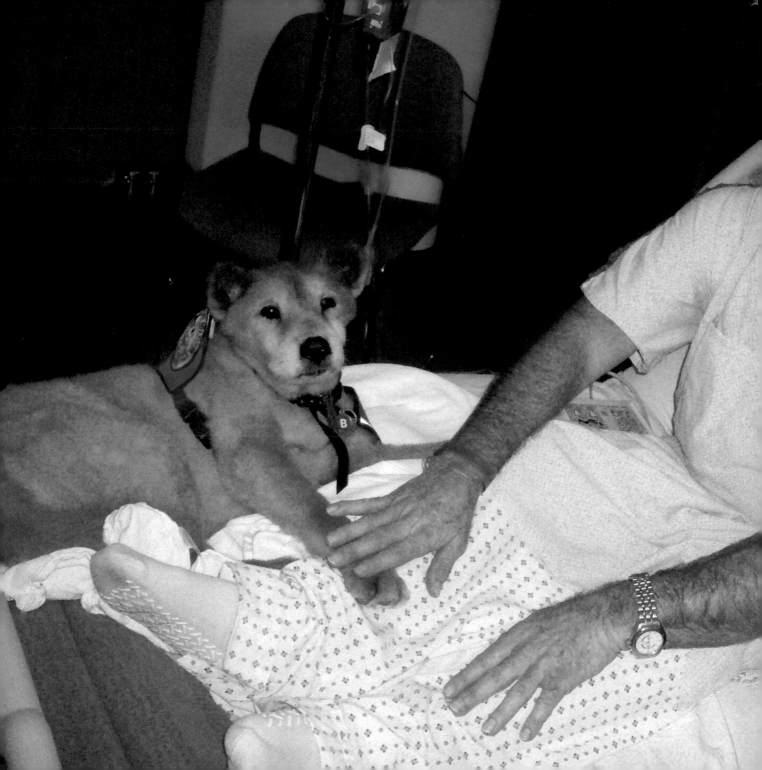

THE POWER
OF
TOUCH

Jan, a nurse, walks over to Baxter. "Baxter, I think you can help with one of my patients. Mike has MS as well as several other debilitating ailments and diseases. He's blind, almost deaf, and his legs are paralyzed. He is sixty-two and totally alone except for one daughter, who visits infrequently.

He's depressed and almost never speaks. Baxter, I'm desperate to get through to him, and I really think you might be able to bring some comfort to Mike. You go in there, boy, and see what miracles you can make happen. Mike would appreciate it, and so would I."

"By the way, speak to him in his right ear. He can hear a little in that ear and zero in the other."

In room 103, with Baxter at my side, I walk over to Mike's right side.

I yell in the only ear that functions. "Mike, I brought Baxter, my therapy dog, to see you. Do you like dogs?"

That one word, "dogs," catapults Mike back to another time in his life, a time when he was a little boy—healthy, innocent, and happy. All of a sudden he is no longer a man, dying, paralyzed and helpless; instead he has become a little boy, alive, full of delight and energy. He sits up strong and has that innocent, quizzical look on his face. I just know he wants to meet Baxter.

"You mean they let you bring dogs in here? Aren't you going to get in trouble? How did you get him in here without someone seeing him?"

"Baxter works here. They know he's here."

"What time does he get off duty?"

"He doesn't have a set schedule."

He bends down to talk to Baxter.

"Mike is a prisoner in his bed. He's locked in his body and you must do what you can to bring a smile to his face, to touch him, to engage him. I know you can help him. Please, Baxie, pull him away from his loneliness."

Baxter watches me speak to him. His ears perk up as he hears my familiar baby talk, only this time I'm begging him to make a difference . . . just for a moment.

Mike feels for the items on his tray to make sure they are where they're supposed to be. Here's the lineup: a lamp, which is on; a carafe; a coffee mug; an inhaler; tissues; and a bell.

I move the tray to the side and put Baxter on the side of Mike's good ear. Maybe Baxter will want to talk to him. He strokes Baxter and becomes surprisingly talkative.

"I used to have a dog. His name was Buster."

He proceeds to tell stories about his dog.

He laughs; we laugh. He smiles; we smile.

"How old is Baxter? What does he look like? Does he like his job? Where does he sleep?"

He touches Baxter, and Baxter licks him.

But Mike yells out, "Stop licking me!"

The solution is to reverse Baxter's position, especially since Mike can't see. I turn Baxter around and put his fluffy tail by Mike's hand.

He strokes Baxter incessantly and asks more and more questions. Sometimes he calls him Buster. I never correct him.

I remember what Jan told me: *Mike is agitated and laconic. Help.*

We allow Mike to pet Baxter for some time. Because we feel that he's enjoying Baxter, we want to indulge him with as many moments with Baxter as possible.

When we leave, we tell him when we will return.

"Today is the fourteenth and we'll be here again on the seventeenth, in three more days. Baxter will come back to see you."

WITH HIS HEIGHTENED SENSE OF TOUCH, BAXTER HELPS MIKE TO GET IN TOUCH WITH LOVE. DURING THESE MOMENTS WITH BAXTER, BAXTER TAKES HIM AWAY FROM HIS ALONENESS.

Mike sits up more. He presses the sheets with his hands. I think he's going to clap, but he doesn't. A smile lights his face.

With his heightened sense of touch, Baxter helps Mike to get in touch with love. During these moments with Baxter, Baxter takes him away from his aloneness.

Mike embraces a relationship with Baxter by both engaging in conversation about him and making physical contact with something that is alive. Baxter is at the center of Mike's life for these moments. At last he has something to touch besides the lineup on his tray table.

We return on the seventeenth, but as Baxter heads toward Mike's room, Jan stops us.

"Mike was never as happy as when you brought Baxter to his room and put him next to him."

She cries. We cry. Mike was special. He was more helpless than any other patient I have ever seen thus far.

Jan adds, "The only time I saw Mike smile was when he was touching Baxter. It was the only time that he really talked."

We remember what Mike said the last time we saw him. Looking straight ahead, looking at no one, with Baxter cuddled up to him, he said, "No one should have to live like this. I'm so stranded in my own body with my diseases."

I am grateful that he was unable to see my tears or how my lips trembled.

I reached out and placed my hand on top of his and bent over and hugged him. Although he was sixty-two, he seemed like a child in bed with his real, live teddy bear.

As Jan said: "Thank God for Baxter."

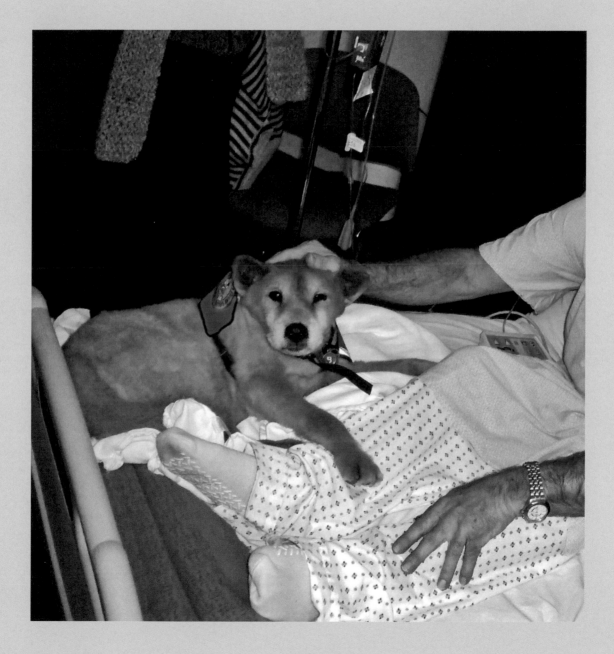

TEN BUSINESS

CARDS

Carla is reading a book as she sits by her mother's bedside. Carolyn, her mother, lies with eyes closed, and her face is smooth. A collection of Robert Frost poems sits open on her chest.

"Hello. Would you like to see a therapy dog?"

"Mom, a dog is here. Would you like to see him?"

"Yes."

"How about if I place him on your mother's bed so that you can pet him, too?"

"Yes, do that," says Carla.

"I LOVE THIS PHOTO WITH BAXTER BECAUSE IT'S LIKE HE'S TEACHING ME ONE OF LIFE'S LESSONS."

I place Baxter close enough to Carolyn that she can pet him if she would like.

Carolyn can't resist him. "Oh, look at him. Isn't he cute?" She pets his head with one hand; the other gets lots of kisses from Baxter.

Carolyn is now fully awake. She asks, "How old is Baxter?"

"He's a lot older than you, I'm sure. He's around ninety-three."

"I'm ninety-one."

"No way. I thought you were around seventy. Neither of you look your age."

"He looks like a puppy."

"Well, just in the face. Baxter is pretty famous. He was on TV on July 19, 2007, when he accompanied a hospice patient to see the new Harry Potter movie. Look, here's one of his business cards."

Carolyn looks it over carefully. "This is really a nice card and a wonderful picture of Baxter. I would like more of these."

"How many is more?"

"Ten!"

"Mom, what will you do with them?"

"Maybe I'll pass them around or just keep them for myself."

I try not to laugh as I take out ten more cards from the pocket of Baxter's therapy jacket. "Here you go."

Dr. Maria walks in. She admires Baxter in bed with the patient. "Baxter is wonderful, isn't he? He's like a person in a dog's body. I imagine him unzipping his fur jacket and out pops a human being."

We decide to leave so Carolyn and Carla can visit with Dr. Maria.

We'll never know what Carolyn did with those ten business cards.

We do know, though, what she thought of his photo.

"I love this photo with Baxter because it's like he's teaching me one of life's lessons."

MS.

VANCOUVER

"Oh my God, I miss my dog so much!"

The woman from Vancouver, British Columbia, drops to the floor and cuddles with Baxter. She is oblivious to anything else around her. Baxter is the aphrodisiac that captures her heart and brings her to her knees. He's irresistible.

"Would you come back with me to see someone?" She says this to Baxter, almost waiting for him to respond.

He follows her to a room. People are everywhere, maybe eight of them. Some are standing near the doorway and some are sitting. There's a range of folks, an eclectic group from hippie to nun. They come from all over, from Vancouver to Dublin, Ireland.

The man in the bed is handsome, with thick salt-and-pepper hair and a trimmed beard. The room is dark, though it is daylight. The stargazer lilies lend a desirable aroma.

> HE HAS MADE SOME SORT OF MYSTERIOUS TRANSITION, AND BAXTER IS NOW PART OF HIS INNER CIRCLE. THEY REALLY DO SEEM TO UNDERSTAND ONE ANOTHER IN A WAY THAT WORDS CANNOT EXPLAIN.

"Would you like Baxter in bed with you?"

"Oh, I just love animals. Yes, put him right here. This side, please, because my leg on the other side is hurting. I can only see shadows, so I can't completely see him."

The room grows silent. Friends look on as I lift Baxter and gingerly place him beside Tom, who immediately responds as if he's before an audience. He begins recanting childhood stories. "I used to rescue dogs and always had a dog growing up.

"Don't you remember?" he asks Ms. Vancouver, the woman who brought Baxter to Tom's room.

As Baxter and Tom exchange love licks and pats, Ms.Vancouver becomes Annie Leibovitz, snapping away at the most handsome pair in the room:

Baxter and Tom. They look like they belong together. Another friend takes a photo with his cell phone. Ms. Vancouver, barefoot, crunches her agile body on the sofa to get a better photo for her memories.

Tom is on autopilot, reminiscing as he holds Baxter like his baby. His fan club is listening intently, but all eyes seem to be on Baxter.

Tears stream down Tom's face as he holds on to Baxter. His voice becomes softer, almost inaudible, so his friends must move in closer. He continues to stroke Baxter, now speaking only to him.

Again the camera phones are firing away, and Ms. Vancouver has moved from the sofa to Tom's bed. He takes the large cross that adorns his concave chest and presses it against Baxter. He struggles to put the cross around Baxter's neck but can't maneuver the task. No one, though, reaches out to help him. It's a moment between Tom and Baxter.

He shocks all in the room by what he says next.

"I feel closer to this dog than to any of you."

I attempt to hold back my tears as I try to fully digest the impact of Tom's words. As I look around the room, everyone except for Baxter is crying. At first, I'm afraid they are offended by this statement, but then I realize that they understand the passage Tom is making. And as we all recognize this, we all smile at Baxter. He seems to smile back, revealing his missing tooth.

We are evidently now farther away from Tom's awareness. He has made some sort of mysterious transition, and Baxter is now part of his inner circle. They really do seem to understand one another in a way that words cannot explain. Tom's friends honor and respect this connection between him and Baxter.

DR. LOVE
— MEETS —
DR. CHAD

Many people think that hospice is all lachry-
mose and dark, but we can have fun. Baxter
is often the vehicle that allows us to cut up and make
people laugh.

This day I spot a bright yellow stethoscope hanging from the door handle at the nurses' station.

"Do you mind if I borrow this?"

Obviously not a real stethoscope, it is ideal for Baxter. I drape it around his neck and he is instantaneously transformed into Dr. Love.

Dr. Chad, stethoscope around his neck, hovers over a patient's file. Dr. Love, stethoscope in his ears, approaches.

"Doctor, do you mind if Dr. Love listens to your heart?"

I place the end of the stethoscope inside Dr. Chad's madras shirt.

"Oh, Dr. Chad, Dr. Love says that you have a lot of love in your heart. You're going to live a long, long time and give this love to many, many people. Dr. Love has unlimited love and this gives him the authority to check the love levels in other people."

Dr. Chad turns to Baxter, cheek to cheek, "I love you, Baxter. And you smell so good."

"I love you, too, Dr. Chad. And, you smell okay, but you would smell even better if you went out and rolled in the grass."

> "DR. LOVE, I HAVE A PATIENT FOR YOU. THE LADY IN THE NEXT ROOM IS DYING OF A BROKEN HEART. SHE MISSES HER HUSBAND WHO RECENTLY DIED HERE AT HOSPICE."

"Dr. Love, I have a patient for you. The lady in the next room is dying of a broken heart. She misses her husband who recently died here at hospice. "

"Well, Dr. Love can try to fix that."

We go into Sarah's room, stethoscope ready.

"Hello, Sarah, Dr. Love's here to check your love levels. Would you like him next to you in bed?"

"I don't think so."

"Okay, then, Dr. Love will just pull up a chair and check your wrist since he can't reach your heart.

"Oh, Sarah, it looks really good for you. You have plenty of love in your heart. You should feel better shortly, just as soon as you realize that. Just keep feeling that love."

Sarah pets Baxter's face and his paws that are hanging over the edge of her bed. Her face brightens up, her lips turn upward, and a smile appears.

"You're really something. You're special," she says.

"You know, Sarah, maybe the next time we visit, you'll be up for Baxter getting in bed with you. That's where he's most effective."

"He's helping me right where he is."

Days later, we're in a room, and Kathleen, one of the nurses, hands me a sticky note with 107 written on it.

"The patient in 107 needs Baxter's love."

I smile. "That must be Sarah."

We return to Sarah's room where I place Baxter in a chair supported by pillows. Sarah reaches over to feel Baxter.

"I missed Baxter. I wanted to see him again."

She touches him. As she moves her arm, I can see underneath it a framed photograph of a man. She is grieving; nonetheless, she gets real pleasure and comfort from seeing and being with Baxter.

Baxter stays there for quite a while until it is time for his dinner and evening walk.

"Baxter will see you in a couple of more days, Sarah. I hope you're home by then, but, if not, Baxter will check on you."

"Bye-bye, Baxter, and thank you for coming."

POPPY
AND
PUPPY

Baxter walks up to a young woman who sits on the edge of a rocking chair in the lounge. Her body drops down to touch him as her voice rises upward to reach me.

"Are you going to 112 now? My dad loves dogs and he's been waiting to see you. Oh, please come to his room."

As we enter her father's room, she says, "Look, Poppy, the puppy has come to see you. Open your eyes, Poppy, and look at the puppy. Oh, Poppy, feel the puppy, feel Baxter. Isn't he soft?"

Her father does not open his eyes; however, his arms and hands envelop Baxter, and Baxter's paws hug Poppy's chest.

The daughter wraps her hands in her father's, creating an octopus of hands and arms all over Baxter. This threesome is bound in love, and the daughter has no way to wipe away her tears.

Dennis asks what kind of music they would like.

"Poppy likes ragtime," suggests a friend of the family's.

Dennis leaves and returns with just the right sound. He places the CD in the player, adjusts the volume, then turns it off. It is not the appropriate time.

"When you're ready for him to listen, it's all ready to go."

"Thank you."

Meanwhile, the relationship between Poppy and puppy unfolds in their silence.

Baxter seems to know that these first moments are the last moments that he will comfort Poppy and his daughter. There's not much air amidst those hugging arms; nonetheless, he stays there for them.

When we return the next day, Poppy is gone, but the ragtime CD is still in the player.

THE DAUGHTER WRAPS HER HANDS IN HER FATHER'S, CREATING AN OCTOPUS OF HANDS AND ARMS ALL OVER BAXTER. THIS THREESOME IS BOUND IN LOVE, AND THE DAUGHTER HAS NO WAY TO WIPE AWAY HER TEARS.

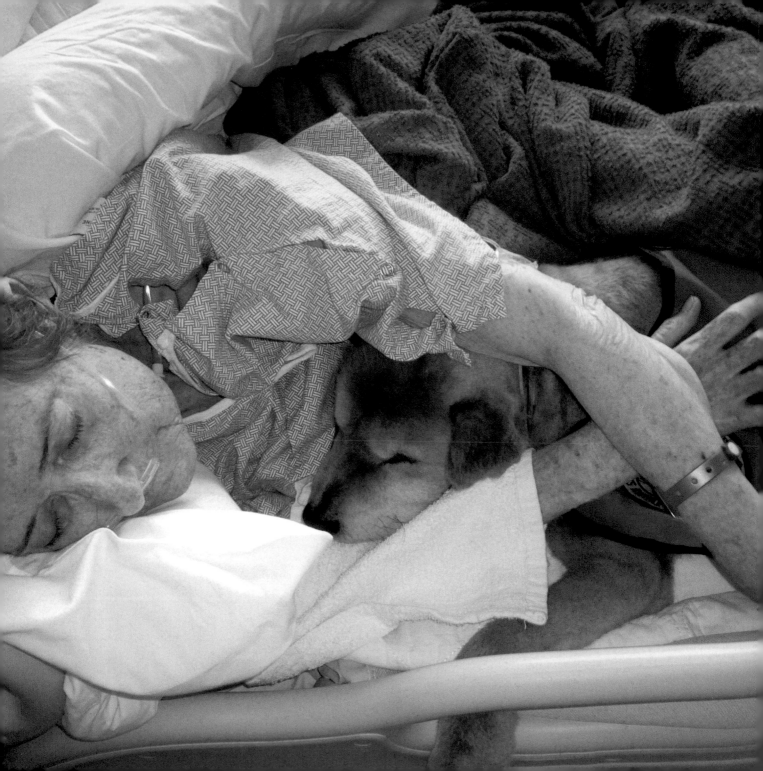

THE ANGEL

OF

HOSPICE

Jean, Joan's sister, shakes her head back and forth as she watches Baxter in bed with her sister, Joan. Baxter's eyes never leave Joan's face as she curls her tiny, frail body around Baxter. She takes both of her arms, spindly as they are, and cradles him. Though her words are brief, in the middle of her squirms she echoes one phrase over and over again: "I love you, Baxter."

"If Baxter could talk Joan, he would say the same back to you. He would say, thank you for loving on me. Thank you for cuddling with me."

Joan's smile melds into Baxter's fur. Jean cries as she bids her sister farewell in her mind. A friend echoes this in the background: "Baxter makes everyone feel better."

Mostly there is silence in the room, except when someone mutters an expression of amazement at Baxter. As Joan rests her lithe body on Baxter, she takes his face and kisses him.

Jean is sitting beside the bed, continuously repeating what becomes a mantra. "He's so precious. Look at those eyes. Look at that face. I can't believe he'll do this for so long. I'm mesmerized."

We all sit very quietly, not talking among ourselves, and let Baxter envelop Joan in his love and touch. This lasts for uncountable moments.

And it is one of these moments that becomes the signature of Baxter's first business card.

Joan's restlessness stops, and she dozes. Baxter remains alert, ready to accommodate her next move, to move in harmony with her.

As we pull Baxter away from Joan, we question to ourselves whether Joan will make it through the night.

Days later we return and at the nurse's station there's a card addressed to Baxter.

San Diego Hospice

Baxter
Certified Therapy Dog

"THE ANGEL OF HOSPICE"

P.O. Box 500341
San Diego, CA 92150-0341
dennis@momentswithbaxter.com

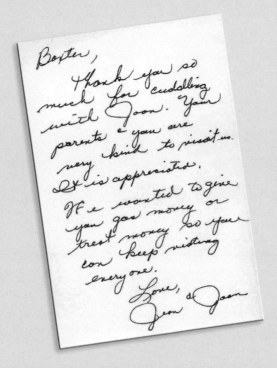

Baxter,

Thank you so much for cuddling with Joan. Your parents & you are very kind to visit us. It is appreciated. If e wanted to give you gas money or treat money so you can keep visiting everyone.

Love,
Leon & Joan

Gloria, one of the certified nurse assistants, adds, "Forty dollars won't fill up my car. You can use that money for Baxter's funeral."

We both laugh.

"Forty dollars won't be enough, Gloria."

"Not enough? You've got to be kidding."

"I'll need about four thousand dollars for his funeral."

"You are crazy about that dog, aren't you?"

"I am."

"I am, too. And everyone else around here is crazy about him. We'll all come to his funeral."

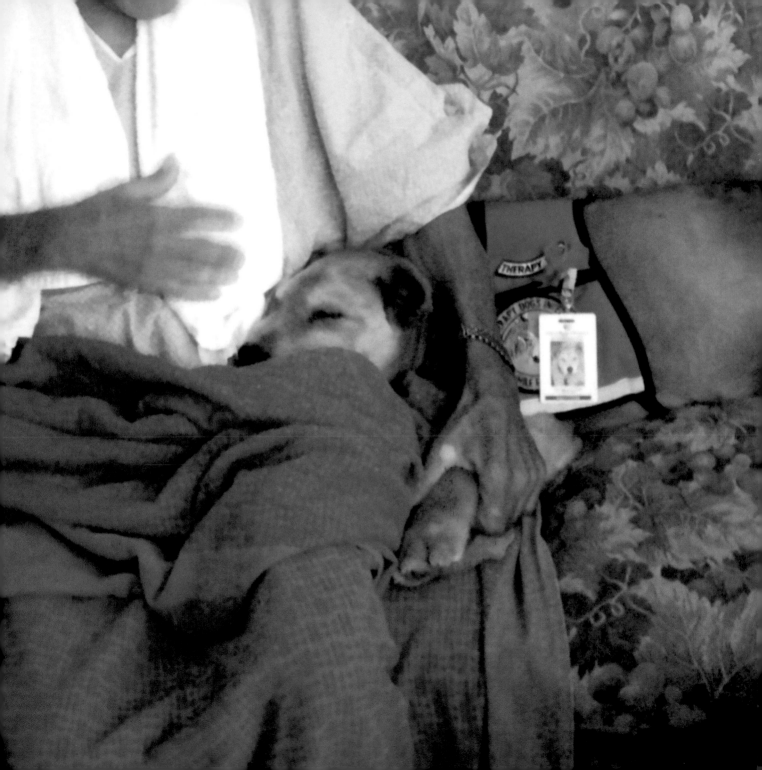

G U S T A V ' S

H U M O R

Gustav is a long, lanky man who wears all-terrain shoes and athletic socks with his hospice gown. Because he's alone, he often walks up and down the halls talking to the staff. He's in a holding pattern: the shoes and socks would take him outside, but the hospice gown and his pain keep him inside, in his room, his only journey one that will take him to the end of his life.

The shoes are hopeful; the gown is disease.

He reminds me of an old Hollywood type, an actor of sorts with a certain presence. He randomly mixes Spanish and English, making it difficult for Dennis and me to follow his conversation. When we do understand him, though, he's very, very funny.

With Baxter, however, the incomprehensible sentences are irrelevant. Gustav is amused with the little guy, and Baxter is our icebreaker. Gus, as the staff calls him, is a little disoriented, but he's upright on his sofa, alone with his disease. I put Baxter on the sofa next to him and he immediately responds.

He strokes Baxter sporadically, asking questions . . . simple ones. "What's his name? How old is he? What kind of dog?" And, last but not least, "Did he fart?"

We all laugh as he waves his hands through the air to deflect the odor. Because I'm sitting by Baxter's rear, I know that it isn't Baxter.

"No, no," I declare adamantly, "Baxter would never fart! It must be you, Gus."

He bursts into laughter, holding his stomach, because that's where he has the pain. We continue to tease each other about who farted, and it becomes a laughing match.

FOR THESE MOMENTS, WITH BAXTER'S FACE ON HIS LAP, GUSTAV'S LAUGHING, HE'S SMILING, HE'S TOUCHING A LIVING THING, AND HE HAS A CERTAIN QUALITY OF LIFE.

As silly as all this might seem, it's essential to remember that Gustav is dying. However, for these moments, with Baxter's face on his lap, he's laughing, he's smiling, he's touching a living thing, and he has a certain quality of life.

And it is Baxter who created this moment.

BABY

GIRL

Baxter is needed to visit a hospice patient who is still at home receiving care from the team.

We arrive in Chula Vista at a yellow and blue house not far from the beach. Rosa, the mom, greets us at the front door. We introduce Baxter and ourselves and she, with all the warmth of a friend, invites us into her home. As I enter, I see Paulita. She sits in a tiny purple chair that's molded to her diminutive body.

She's hooked up to a machine, like a ventilator, on wheels with a short lead that limits her movement but keeps her alive. Her tracheotomy tube makes her speech barely discernable. Though Paulita is bilingual, she speaks only Spanish to Baxter and her mom.

Baxter walks directly over to Paulita. They are the same size.

"If you get me a towel for your sofa, I can put Baxter on it right next to Paulita," I say.

Rosa produces a thick, warm towel. I place Baxter on the towel, then he places his big, furry paws across Paulita's legs. He doesn't move them until we pick him up two hours later.

BAXTER LOOKS DEEPLY INTO EACH PERSON'S EYES AND CREATES A LIGHT IN THE ROOM THAT I ASSUME WILL GLOW LONG AFTER WE DEPART.

Paulita is all over Baxter, fondling him and flicking his ears with his I.D. badge and his business card. He's completely agreeable to whatever this little girl does. She pulls his tail, pats his head, rubs him, and hugs him. She gives him kisses several times. She looks at her mother, who is holding her upright. Paulita smiles big, laughs, and high-fives with her mother.

Paulita has found a new friend, and so has Baxter.

Moments like these are exactly what Paulita, Rosa, and Baxter all need. Paulita clearly loves having Baxter by her side. He remains attentive to her every move and never flinches. He's like a stuffed animal, there for her needs, always obeying.

Even during the many times her mom turns on the loud suction device for the trach tube, Baxter is calm and quiet. This all seems like an ordeal to

"I have a pug, Tuffy. He comes up here, but he's not calm like you. Baxter, you are wonderful! Come here, doll."

Jesse calls everyone he likes "doll," from the nurses to his friends and especially his customers, who visit him regularly.

"My job was to choose fine clothes for men, but my real customers were the wives. And with my garrulous personality, I was able to woo these women into my haberdashery. I became their confidant, sort of like a hairstylist."

"Jesse has fabulous taste. This is just one of the many items he gave me." Emma, Jesse's mother, flashes her hand in front of me so that I can see the ring Jesse bought her.

Jesse lies with Baxter, stroking him while Emma clutches the animation in her son's delivery as he tells his stories. This is the Jesse she will remember.

With each gesticulation, Baxter's eyes follow Jesse's hands as they move in the air, enhancing the comedy of the moment. As his hands come back to Baxter's body, rubbing away, Baxter lays his head in Jesse's lap.

With each visit, Jesse becomes more and more unavailable for Baxter. Now, when we visit, Baxter is there for Emma and oftentimes, Jesse's grandmother, appropriately named Granny.

Since Jesse is no longer talking, Emma takes her conversation to Baxter, who receives her heartily with kisses. Her demeanor instantaneously transforms from a wilting spirit to an uplifted presence when she engages with Baxter.

> THERE WITH BAXTER, EMMA CAN HIDE INSIDE HIS LOVE, WHICH IS A WARM, SOOTHING SALVE THAT COATS THE CRACKS IN HER BROKEN HEART. HIS LOVE FORMS A PROTECTIVE LAYER THAT GIVES EMMA STRENGTH TO FACE THIS TRAGEDY.

us, but to Rosa, it's just become part of being a mommy to Paulita.

During our lengthy visit, we meet Rosa's aunt, mother-in-law, son, and husband. Each one exchanges places with Paulita and has one-on-one time with Baxter. He looks deeply into each person's eyes and creates a light in the room that I assume will glow long after we depart.

Baxter's silence is a loud voice, a voice that speaks to anyone, of any ethnicity, in any language. It knows no boundaries. Baxter's magic is pervasive and palpable.

"Who do you think benefited the most from Baxter?" Dennis asks when we get up to leave.

Paulita's father, Oscar, answers.

"The whole family."

BAXIE'S
BLANKET!

We go in to see Jesse. Though close to death, Jesse almost rises from his bed just to greet Baxter.

Wearing his Prada glasses and a stylish ring, Jesse invites Baxter to his bed by opening his arms. He speaks to Baxter as if he is a longtime pal.

"Hey, Emma, you need some therapy, some relief. Let's go in the common area on the sofa and put Baxter next to you."

Her face brightens as she gives herself permission to leave Jesse's side.

She baby talks with Baxter, and he responds with kisses and places his paws on her leg. They bond there on the sofa like a mother and her baby.

When Granny arrives, I put Baxter in between them.

"Granny, you're almost the same age as Baxter, ninety-two."

She smiles, but not completely. She stops halfway, allowing me to see the sadness that she can't deny. Still, for these moments, she escapes the dread of her grandson leaving the world at fifty.

Emma basks in Baxter's love. She scoops it up, takes it with her, and finds some solace in her communications with Baxter. When she's with Baxter, he allows her to escape her pain. He takes her to another place, where only love, innocence, and joy exist. For these moments, Baxter indulges Emma in his world.

It's as if Emma is in a dream. There with Baxter she can hide inside his love, which is a warm, soothing salve that coats the cracks in her broken heart. His love forms a protective layer that gives Emma strength to face this tragedy. She's now recharged.

Each time Emma sees that Baxter has arrived, she scurries out of Jesse's room and makes a beeline for the sofa. Baxter knows what she wants. He walks toward Emma and I put him next to her. She drapes her body on his and again has her own private conversation with him.

We get to know a little about Emma, moments of her life. She arrives at 9:00 and leaves at 6:30 every day. Hospice is her home away from home.

The last time we see Emma at hospice, the day Jesse dies, she hands me an oversized bag with tissue paper inside bound with a silky beige bow.

"What's this?"

"This is for Baxie." She always chose to call him by his nickname, the name on our license plates. "I know he sleeps with crib sheets and I thought that he just might need this."

"Oh, it's gorgeous. How thoughtful of you! In the midst of what you're enduring, how did you have the wherewithall to even think beyond Jesse?"

"A friend of my daughter sews, and she offered to make this blanket for me to give to you. Some of the dogs in this fabric look just like Baxie."

Tears pool in my eyes and my voice quivers. I wrap myself around Emma just like I will wrap Baxie in his new blanket.

"I love the colors. It's just perfect for Baxter. Now you've brought Baxter just as much warmth as he brings to you."

That blanket has been on Baxie's bed ever since Emma gave it to him.

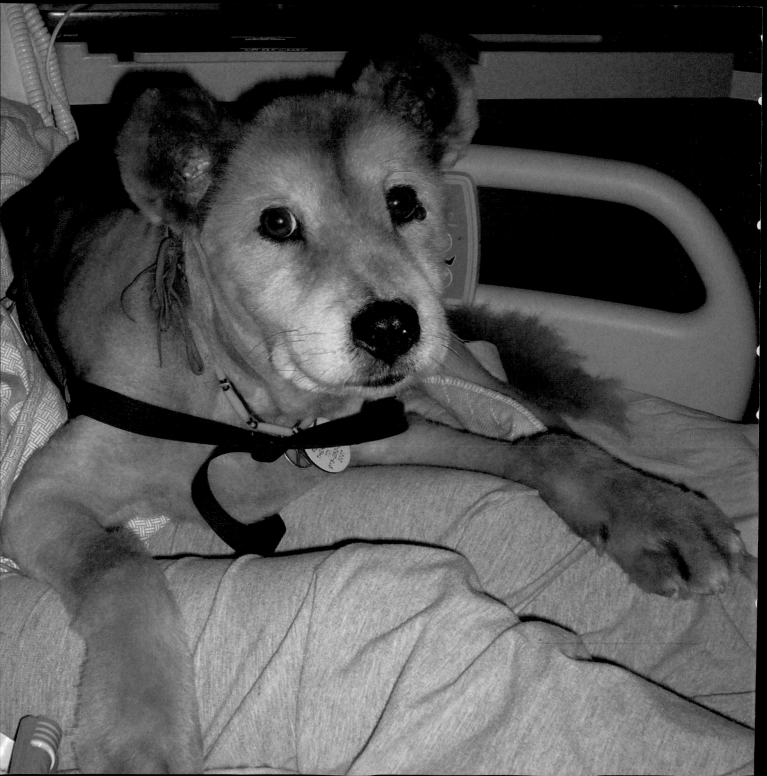

LILLY
AND
HERWIG

Nurse Tim approaches us.

"You must go see Lilly in 109. She's a sweet woman, and I think she would love Baxter. She's all alone."

The three of us, like Dorothy, Toto, and the Cowardly Lion, enter Lilly's room.

She welcomes us into her room, where uneaten food sits on the tray beside her bed. Though the food is beautifully presented, she does not feel like indulging. She has not eaten in days and will not eat again before she dies.

WE CAN TELL THAT BEING WITH BAXTER OCCUPIES HER MIND AND FILLS HER HEART. BECAUSE OF HIM, SHE'S MORE DISTANT FROM HER PAIN AND HER DEATH. HE FILLS THE SPACE WHERE FAMILY BELONGS.

"Put him right here. Oooh, I just love dogs."

Baxter goes right to Lilly as I hand him over. She is on top of the bedspread, wearing a lovely wig. She gets into a fetal position and completely curls herself around Baxter. Both of them are one, in harmony, like yin and yang.

Lilly lies here for a long while and we talk about common ground. Food becomes the subject, and she dreams of the desire to want to eat. She conjures up a scenario where she is eating on her patio, having a bountiful meal of fried chicken.

"It could be baked, fried, broiled, or boiled. I just love chicken. When you guys return, we can all eat it together and give the bones to Baxter."

"I have two daughters, but they both work and they have children. They'll be up here soon."

Tim, though, had earlier told us that they don't visit.

We let her go on and on, and we can tell that being with Baxter occupies her mind and fills her heart. Because of him, she's more distant from her pain and her death. He occupies the space where family belongs.

We visit Lilly one other time. On this day she looks different: she is without her wig. She tells us she wants to be next to Baxter by moving over in her bed. She

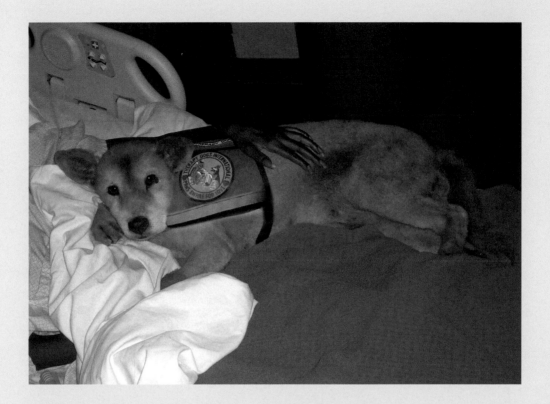

is weaker and less available; nonetheless she has energy for Baxter. I attempt to bring laughter, even though Baxter has already brought a smile to her face. I get a little crazy and put on her wig.

"You need to color your hair and make it look like that wig," Lilly says.

I take her advice, and the next week I get highlights put in my hair. My intention is to return to Lilly's bedside and show her that I followed through on her suggestion.

Baxter heads toward Lilly's room to introduce my new look, but Lilly is no longer there.

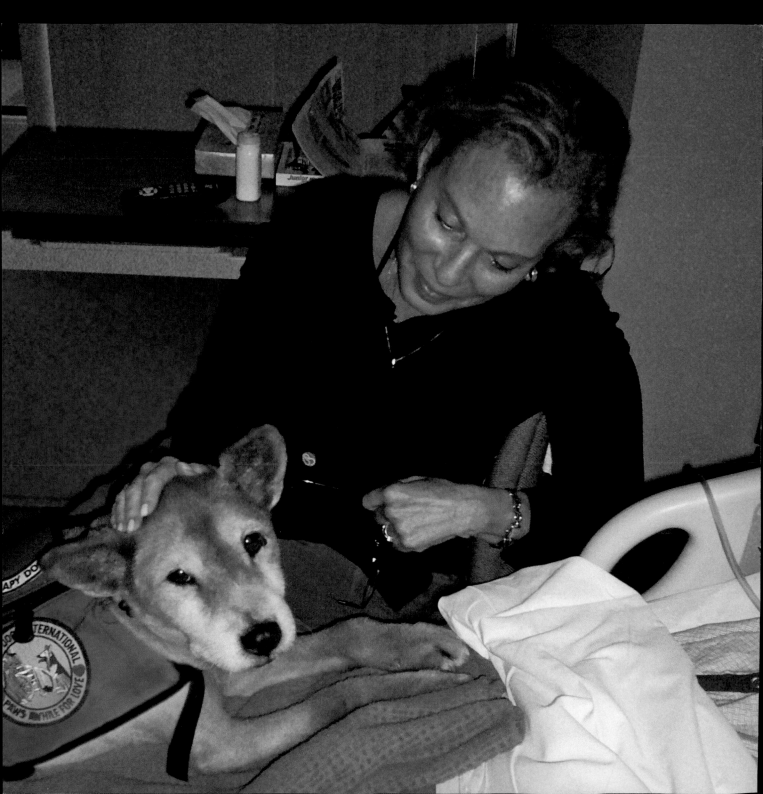

MO'S

LAST DAY

As we enter hospice, Sara, one of the nurses, approaches Baxter and me.

"One of your friends is back here. Mo has returned here to die. You're not going to like it, so be prepared. She looks different. She's unresponsive. And, she's in a lot of pain, especially her legs. We can't move her, as she screams out if we touch her legs. She's comfortable, though, if we just let her be. However, she's imminent."

I get this awkward, heavy feeling in my gut and tears well up in my eyes.

"Oh, my God, I'm so sorry to hear this, but I'm so grateful she's here. This is a wonderful place for her to die."

"I CAN'T BELIEVE THIS. THIS IS MAGICAL. BAXTER IS MAGICAL."

Sara continues, "Kathy, her niece, is keeping vigil by Mo's side. She never leaves. You and Baxter can go see her. I'm sure she would really like to see Baxter. She's in 211."

"Sara, thanks for letting me know this. I'll go get Dennis and we'll go see her right now."

We enter Mo's room, darkened by the spirit and the closed accordion blinds. Kathy is completely beside herself. She's alone in her thoughts, alone with Mo, and alone in her grief.

When she sees Baxter walk in, however, her eyes open wide, she lifts her head, the corners of her mouth move upward, and she holds out her hand to greet him. She's overjoyed to have this elixir of love grace Mo's room.

"Hello Baxter, am I glad to see you!" She welcomes us with open arms, giving us all hugs. We visit with her for a while, letting her rattle on and on about little things in her life that don't pertain to Mo. She's edgy and just needs to talk.

I peer at Mo out of the corner of my eye and am stunned by her appearance. I don't say anything, but I don't look for long. "Hello, Mo. Baxter is here to see you." Without Baxter, I would be at a loss for what to do next.

"Kathy, what do you think about putting Baxter in bed with Mo? That's how they both remember each other and I think it might be effective."

"That's a wonderful idea. Let's try that."

I lower the rail of the bed to create more room for Baxter. I must not let Baxter touch Mo's body, especially her legs, or he will cause her great pain. I place Baxter next to her. His legs are hanging off the bed, so I support him with my leg as I sit in a chair right beside him. He seems to know it's Mo. He stares at her. Then, he just rests his head between his paws and continues to look at her.

All of a sudden, before any of us can react, Baxter gets up and lies down across Mo's legs. I'm watching with disbelief. I signal to Kathy and Dennis.

"Hey, you guys, look at Baxter and Mo."

They both turn their heads and, like me, are in complete amazement. Their mouths open and we all just stare.

"I've got to get Fawn, Mo's nurse," Kathy says.

"No, I'll get her," Dennis replies.

None of us needs to go anywhere, because Fawn enters just then to check on Mo. She, too, is shocked.

"No one has been able to touch Mo," Fawn claims. She leaves to gather the other nurses.

They enter along with a social worker, Barbara, and a volunteer. "I can't believe this. This is magical. Baxter is magical," Barbara says with a quiver to her voice.

This goes on for some time as we all shake our heads and watch the beauty of this moment, a moment that is just what Kathy needs.

Kathy stares at her aunt. "Maybe Mo has been waiting for this moment with Baxter before she can die."

With that, I remove Baxter from Mo's body and I turn and walk away.

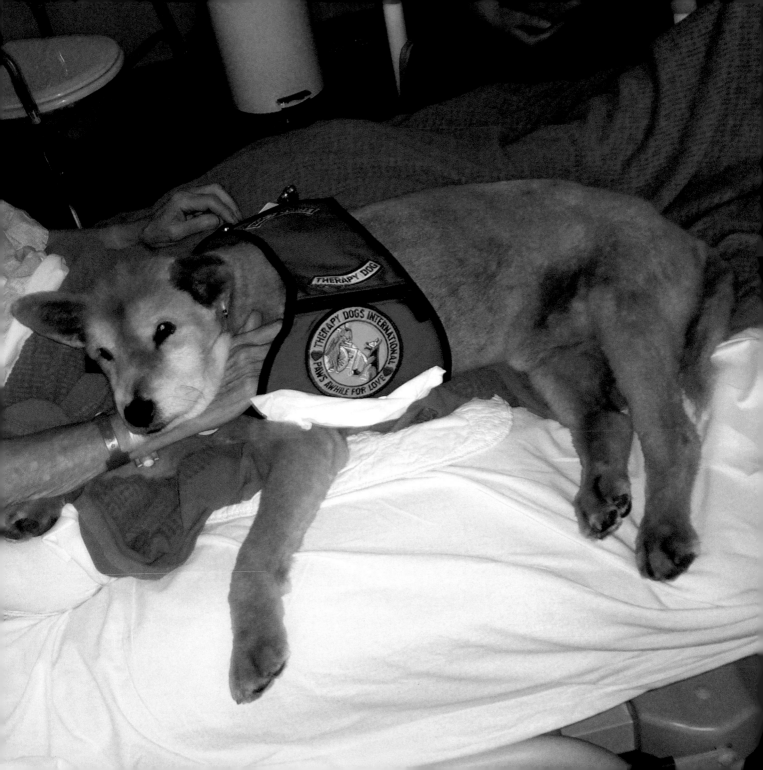

THE BLIND

CAN SEE

Will and Sally have been a team for over fifty years. While Will is lying in bed, Sally shuffles around the room doing all that she can for her husband. This is not unusual for Sally; she's been helping Will for many, many years.

"Hello, how would you guys like to meet Baxter, the therapy dog?"

"Oh, come right in. We'd love to meet him." Sally speaks for both herself and Will.

"Would it be okay if I put him next to you in bed?"

"Sure."

"Here we go then."

Will immediately connects, with his whole body turned toward Baxter's.

"I had a seeing-eye dog for seventeen years," Will explains. "I've been blind since I was in my teens. My wife, Sally, has explained everything in the world to me while we've traveled. I can assure you that I have missed nothing. I have seen more than you, even with my blind eyes.

"Hey, boy, tell me something about you. Yeah, you're such a good dog. Do you love your mama? I bet you do. And your papa, too. Yeah, come here, boy, and let me love on you.

"Now, tell me how old you are. Do you like your job?"

Baxter never moves his eyes away from Will's. Baxter communicates through his devotion to this moment, with this patient. He's attuned to Will's voice and all his warmth. Baxter returns the attention by putting his paws on Will's chest, licking his hand, and keeping his ears perked to listen to every word Will utters.

WILL IS TALKING AWAY WITH BAXTER. THE TWO OF THEM ARE HAVING THEIR OWN PRIVATE CONVERSATION. IF YOU LISTEN REALLY HARD, I THINK THAT YOU CAN HEAR THEM.

Every now and again, Sally chimes in to emphasize Will's love for animals.

"I love them, too. We've had dogs most of our married life."

"There's a picture window over my kitchen sink," Will says, "and every morning Sally and I look out at the birds and flowers and she describes the minutest detail of each flower, each bird, and the colors everywhere. I see it all with her aid. She has done this all of our married life. Sally is my eyes."

"And Will is all of my heart."

Will turns toward Sally. "Honey, tell me what Baxter looks like."

"Oh, he has the cutest face you'll ever see. He has the coloring of our dog Jake. You know, that reddish color intermixed with blond. He has eyeliner surrounding his eyes as if it were tattooed on. His eyes are brownish golden, and they are deep. He looks at you with a special intensity."

"He has a wet black nose to complement that black eyeliner, and his ears are too big for his face. They rest in the up position and they're covered in cinnamon fur. Just feel them, Will. His paws are large, more for a big dog. And, he has a photo I.D. He's just adorable."

"Okay, now I see him. Explain to me this jacket he's wearing." Will tugs on Baxter's vest.

"It's his uniform, which indicates he's a therapy dog. Here, feel these emblems. That one says 'therapy dog.' Now feel this patch. It's blue and circular and has a person in a wheelchair with two dogs at his feet. One is a golden retriever; the other, a German shepherd. On the patch it says 'Paws Awhile for Love.' And that's just what Baxter does."

Will laughs. "You can say that again."

We are interrupted by the telephone. Will and Baxter both turn toward the sound. "Who's that, Baxter? What's that, boy?"

Baxter's ears are on high alert. He turns his head to communicate with Will.

"Honey, answer the phone," Will says to Sally.

"I'm getting there."

It takes her six rings to make it. Her short pant legs reveal cuffed white socks and brown shoes. I just want to hug her as she scurries to the phone.

"Hello! Oh, you won't believe what we're doing. Baxter, a therapy dog, is in bed with Will. Will is talking away with Baxter. The two of them are having their own private conversation. If you listen really hard, I think that you can hear them."

Baxter, Dennis, and I decide to leave to allow them to have their time talking on the phone. As we leave, Sally and Will wave good-bye to Baxter . . . forever.

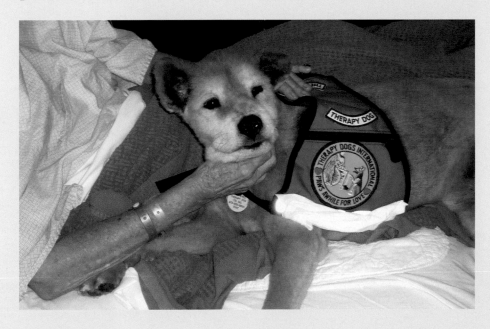

BAXTER
OPENS
THE DOOR

Donna is standing in the hallway, but just barely. The wall behind her is her only support. Baxter sniffs out her pain and walks right up to her.

"Would you like to be with Baxter, or would someone in your room like to be with Baxter?"

"I don't think so. My mom's not doing well." Donna sniffles and wipes her cried-out eyes.

"Well, maybe Baxter would help."

She responds, but her words are muddled by her sobbing.

Baxter follows her to her blow-up bed. Donna collapses on the bed, and Baxter nuzzles inside her arms as she begins to wail. She holds Baxter firmly, and he licks her tears. The more he licks, the more she cries. I leave them like this until she begins to contain herself, her tears subside, and she focuses on Baxter instead of her sadness.

Her mom, Virginia, lies in the bed, curled up in a fetal position, dwindling in both body and spirit. Donna, though, is full of life and animation as she becomes entranced with Baxter. He is the perfect palliative for her pain.

WE WANT TO COMFORT DONNA WITH BAXTER, TO EASE HER PAIN. SHE LETS US IN, BUT IT IS BAXTER WHO OPENS THE DOOR.

"I've been camping out here for days. I want to give back all the love my mother has given me over the years. I won't leave her side. In fact, I'd better get back to my mom now. Thank you, Baxter, for comforting me."

"Baxter will visit you again. And maybe the next time, your mom will be able to meet him and we can put him in bed next to her."

"Okay, that would be very nice if she's able. I just don't know."

There is a next time, and Virginia luxuriates in Baxter's affection. She has a personal conversation with Baxter and speaks in baby talk to him, not unlike the way she does with her own dog, Feebie.

"I'm so worried about Feebie. Who will care for him? He's been with me for so long and I just don't know how he'll be without me." She hugs Baxter as she agonizes over her own dog.

"Mom, I will take Feebie. Don't worry about him."

Virginia, though close to her death, continues to be a mother to Donna.

"Donna, you have all the tools you need. It's Feebie that can't manage by himself." Donna is a grown woman, independent, self-sufficient, therefore able to care for herself. Feebie, Virginia's dog, is completely dependent.

"I know, Mom. Nick and I will take Feebie."

Virginia continues to talk about her life experiences, all the while embracing Baxter. She tells us how she was in this same location in a facility for tuberculosis. "You know I've been here before. Well, not this same building, but this same address, back in the sixties."

Donna is having a tough time remaining unemotional as she watches her mom engage with Baxter.

Virginia begins to fall asleep with Baxter in her arms. I ease Baxter away, and behind me, Donna reaches out to hug Baxter and me. "Thank you for coming," she says.

She, like her mom, speaks baby talk with Baxter. She kisses him on his nose and whispers words of appreciation. She cries again. She knows the end is near.

We go back several more times, but it becomes more about Donna than about her mother. We want to comfort her with Baxter, to ease her pain. She lets us in, but it is Baxter who opens the door.

THE

SOOTHSAYER

Kathleen, one of the nurses, hands me a piece of paper with "102 please" written on it. Though Baxter has been working all day, we decide to take him to one more room. It is New Year's Day, and we are aware that holidays at hospice can be lonely.

The three of us walk in and find Patricia alone. She is like a movie star, dressed to appeal to others. She sits on the edge of her bed in a soft white robe, untied to reveal her pink lacy nightgown. She wears fluffy slippers and tall socks. Her nails are perfectly manicured, long and pink, and her makeup looks to have been applied by an artist. Several tubes feeding her with pain medication stream from under her gown. The tubes, though, are hidden inside a large, fancy black bag that she must tote whenever she moves around the room.

I notice a mirror beside her bed, as well as a makeup bag. She's dressed to live, not to die.

"Hello, Patricia. Would you like to meet my therapy dog?"

"A dog? Where is he?" Her voice seems snappy. Baxter trails in, and I pick him up and put him at the foot of her bed.

"Oh, poor baby. You're old and sick. You're suffering. I can tell; I know. I know because I'm suffering. Baxter isn't healthy," she says to me. As she tells me this, she looks up with her puppy-dog brown eyes accented with mascara and tattooed brows.

"He's in pain. He's ready for the other side, just like me. He understands about death, and he understands me."

Dennis and I listen as she rambles on about Baxter, death, her husband, and being in a world of desperate housewives. I want to cover Baxter's ears when she becomes psychic about his demise as well as her own. I want to protect him from

> "BAXTER IS BEAUTIFUL. HE HAS BEAUTIFUL MARKINGS. HE KNOWS NOTHING OF WHAT HE LOOKS LIKE. HE'S FREE OF ALL THAT. HE LIVES FROM THE INSIDE."

her predictions. But maybe she's right. Maybe she does know something I don't about Baxter.

Baxter coughs.

"He has bronchitis, doesn't he?"

"Yes, he does, because he has a collapsed trachea."

"I have cats at home, three, and I just adore them. They know so much about me and they bring me such comfort. Just like Baxter."

She continues to lean over Baxter and stroke him with her sinewy hands. "Look, our hair is about the same color. Mine's a wig, though. People here, when I arrived, told me that I'm so pretty. I tell them that I just know how to put on makeup better than they. Baxter is beautiful. He has beautiful markings. He knows nothing of what he looks like. He's free of all that. He lives from the inside. I make myself up to make myself feel better. I try to convince myself that I feel well, and getting all fixed up seems to help me. I have another wig in the top drawer over there."

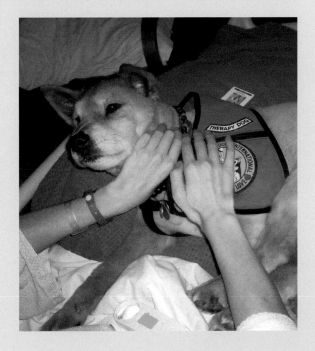

She gets up, dragging her black bag, and I follow beside her. She takes out the wig and places it on Baxter's head. We all start laughing. It feels good to see her laugh, because she is so very sad and alone with her beauty and her disease.

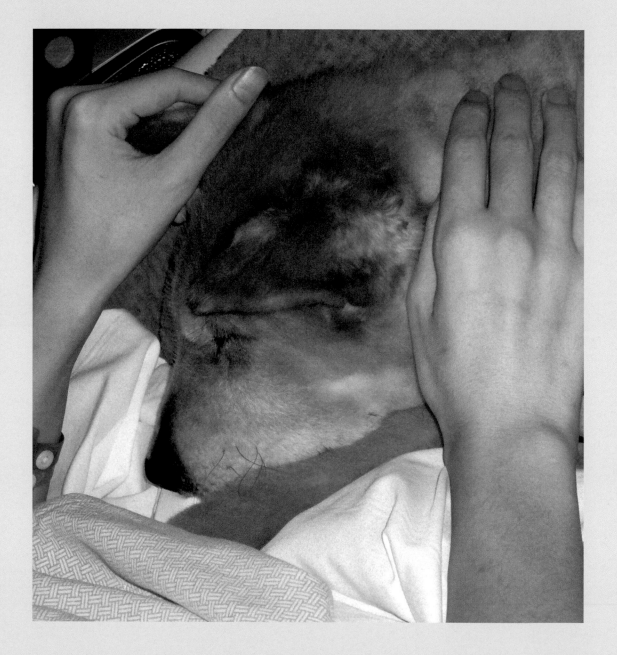

"My husband has cancer, too. He's having surgery in a few days and I'm here dying. My body, though, is not part of my soul. My body will die and my soul will continue. I know this."

"You know, Patricia, you could set up a table here with a crystal ball. Instead of your wig, you could wear a turban. You're perfect for the job."

She laughs out loud and continues to rub Baxter. "I know these things because I'm so close to death. Just like Baxter."

I'm starting to believe her.

"Patricia, what kind of music do you like?"

"I'm a classical aficionado. I have walls of music in my home."

Dennis tells her that he will return with some selections for her.

She goes through the stack. "I don't want the Wagner or the Verdi. It's too much like marching music. I'll take the Bach, Beethoven, and Brahms."

Dennis plays Brahms and she knows all the pieces. She seems unsettled, though. She moves around, changing her position, never quite getting in the bed. She constantly rearranges her hair as it crosses her cheeks.

"The food is really good here. Did you know that? I love the soups. They're homemade."

"Yes, we've eaten here many times."

She looks over at the clock. "It's about time for them to bring my meal."

"Yes, and we're about to leave."

She stands up, and I walk over to give her a big hug.

"Nice cashmere sweater," she whispers in my ear.

Dennis waves good-bye and I lift Baxter to give her a kiss.

"We'll see you next time," I say, wishing it were true.

BAXTER
THE
KING

We take Baxter to hospice on all holidays— Valentine's Day, Halloween, St. Patrick's Day—even those that don't seem so significant. Thanksgiving is particularly wonderful at hospice, because family and friends are everywhere. This is a big day for Baxter. He knows that the

EVERYONE IS SMILING,
AND THAT
INCLUDES BAXTER.
IT'S A WIN-WIN
SITUATION,
BECAUSE NOW THE
PATIENT CAN TOUCH
BAXTER AND HE CAN
TOUCH HER.

more people he touches, the more people come in touch with love and joy.

I tap on the door of our first patient. "Hello, is anyone here interested in meeting Baxter, a therapy dog?"

As I peek in, I am greeted with smiles and a "Yes, please come in."

Three people are in the room: a ninety-two-year-old patient, her daughter, and her son-in-law.

"This is Baxter."

He walks in with a dignified air, the way of an elder who knows his place in this room, in any room, with anyone.

The patient is sitting up in a high chair-like contraption and is just finishing her turkey and dressing. I make the necessary introductions, and the daughter repeats to her mother everything that I say. "I would really like to get Baxter closer to your mother. She really can't experience the wonders of Baxter without being engaged with him. I know this is a rather wild idea."

"Oh, no, I'm willing to try anything for my mother. She adores dogs."

"Okay, then. May I use that pillow over there?"

She nods and again smiles.

I place the pillow on the table part of the patient's chair. The chair is all one piece, connected and strong. Then I pick up all thirty-seven pounds of Baxter and place him on the pillow, where Thanksgiving dinner had been.

"Baxter is accustomed to being up high like this. He's the king in our world, and now he's on a throne in your room."

Everyone is smiling, and that includes Baxter. It's a win-win situation, because now the patient can touch Baxter and he can touch her. She immediately strokes him and he watches her with eyes that melt her soul. He's right there in her face and, though her vision and hearing are not sharp, he's so close that none of this matters. She can see all of him and what she misses, she can easily touch.

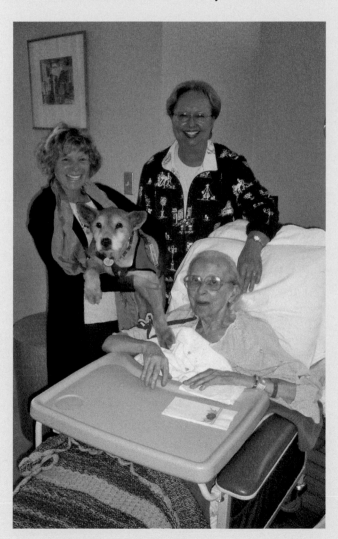

The family is entranced by the patient–dog connection.

"Did you know that Baxter is older than you? I hear that you're ninety-two, but Baxter is ninety-five. He's just the right age for you."

Everyone laughs.

"This is so fantastic! Could we get a photo of my mom and me and Baxter?"

With their camera, Dennis captures this moment. He doesn't have to ask them to smile. They are already happy with Baxter. You would never know that someone in the photo is dying.

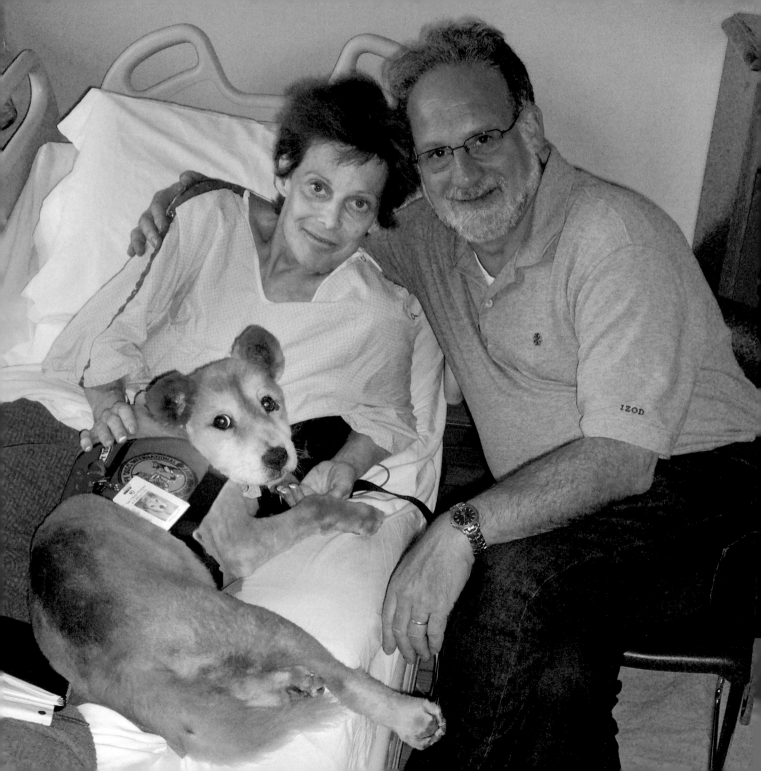

STEPHEN

SMILES

Stephen invites Baxter into Marguerite's room with an uncertain look. He makes the sleeping sign, clasped hands to his tilted face, but still motions for Baxter to enter. Baxter seems to understand and walks slowly toward Stephen's sister's bed.

"I know Marguerite wants Baxter beside her."

Marguerite is without her funky headband, her bald head exposed.

"Look, Marguerite, do you notice anything different about Baxter?" I say, as I arrange Baxter so that his warm body can feel hers. "See, he's bald like you. I shaved his head in honor of you. He wants to have a partner in crime."

BAXTER IS THE HAND **THAT CONNECTS** BROTHER AND SISTER.

She smiles. Stephen smiles. We all smile. It is a good thing.

Marguerite attempts to cradle Baxter, bracing his bony back from the bed rail.

Marguerite has few words for Baxter. As with Baxter, her words are in her eyes. She can readily identify with his ways of loving her, and she communicates her love in stroking, grabbing, and repositioning. She turns to her brother and smiles. He smiles in response. When Marguerite angles her body, we can see that her iridescent eyes match his.

Her fingers graze Baxter's eyelids, her hands cup his face toward hers for a kiss, his paws rest on her lap, and her hands pet him as she slides them back and forth underneath his little therapy jacket. She clutches his jacket and pulls him in closer. She slides her hands under his rear and turns it just so.

I can hear her though just barely: "There we go, but not quite."

She lifts his chest and rearranges him to be more on her. He's a rag doll, going into any shape she designs.

When Marguerite gets up to go to the restroom, Baxter takes over the warm spot she leaves behind. She returns and whispers something to him, grabbing his paw. His ears flutter as her breath scrapes the fur. She moves onto the sofa and

I bring Baxter over to be beside her. Stephen takes his place between Marguerite and Baxter. Baxter is the hand that connects brother and sister. And Stephen, with his smile still intact, allows Baxter to unfold the moment. Stephen knows this moment will be followed by scant more.

I suggest to Dennis that he turn on some background music. As soon as Marguerite hears it, she offers up a sigh—of relief, of pleasure—and smiles as she continues to cuddle with Baxter. Stephen dozes to recharge from these cherished moments with Baxter and Marguerite.

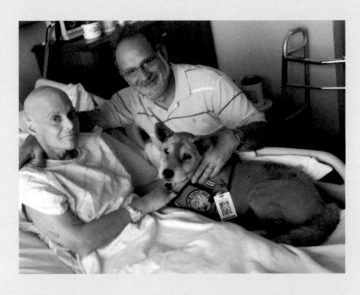

"I got so relaxed. That music and Marguerite holding on to Baxter just felt so good."

"I know you must be very tired traveling every week from Maine to San Diego to see your sister. Just relax."

It's now time for us to go, though we could stay here for hours more. I pull Baxter away from Marguerite's clutch; she holds on for dear life.

"Baxter will be back on Tuesday," I reassure her.

I grab her hand; she squeezes it firmly. I squeeze back. I don't want to let go. I don't know if she will be here next Tuesday, but I give her something to look forward to. I reach for Stephen's extended hand and he smiles at me. He pats Baxter.

Though his lips don't move, I know what he's saying.

BAXTER
MAKES IT
ALL BETTER

B efore I even enter the hallway, the social worker, Daniel, approaches me. "Could you go right away to Room 106? They're doggie people."

"Baxie and I will go now."

I enter the room. I note that there is a collage of dog photos on the armoire doors facing the patient's

> "I THINK THAT BAXTER BROUGHT MY DAD A SENSE THAT IT WAS OKAY TO DIE. AND HE MADE IT OKAY FOR US, TOO."

bed. It makes for a happy ambiance. "Well, I hear you guys all love dogs."

I enter cheerfully and sense that it might be effective if I just put Baxter in bed with this patient, who is in and out of consciousness. He is surrounded by several family members and a friend, all of whom want to do their share to bring him comfort. Smiles light their faces as they watch Baxter put his head on the gentleman's arm.

"Do you think that's too heavy for your father's arm?"

"No, it's fine."

The feel of Baxter awakens the patient, who hasn't uttered a word in twenty-four hours. He immediately purses his lips to try to kiss Baxter. He makes the noise that supposedly dogs identify as "come here." I put Baxter's face closer to his and his face becomes alive. Baxter seems to connect with this patient in ways that his family cannot.

"Oh, how I wish my other son were here! He'll be here shortly and he's a dog lover, just like we are. But more."

Another daughter enters the room and I put Baxter on the sofa so she can cuddle him. She's in heaven, having almost forgotten where she is and what burden she carries. She is smiling, calm, and focused on this moment with Baxter. Baxter is like a baby in her arms. He plays the part well.

"I can see that it's time now to leave. Baxter never wants to wear out his welcome. I'll check back on you later, before we leave for the evening. Maybe your other son can meet Baxter then."

"That would be wonderful. I'll tell him you will return."

I do return, and they are most appreciative, though the son has not yet arrived.

"We'll be back at hospice on Memorial Day. We come on all holidays from Valentine's Day to Halloween, regardless of the significance. I'll check back then."

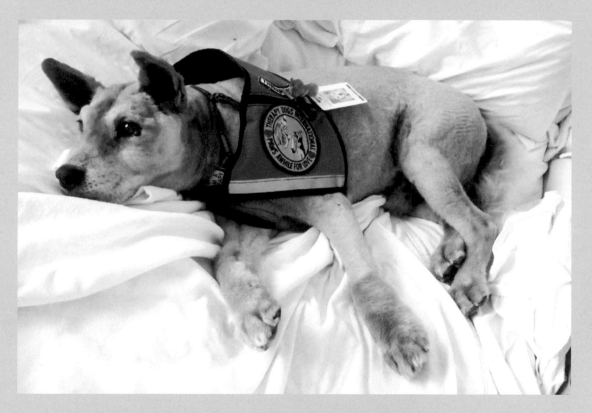

On Memorial Day, the other son comes and fetches us from the hall. "This must be Baxter. I've admired his photos and have wanted to meet him. Do you think you could bring him into my father's room now?"

"Why, of course."

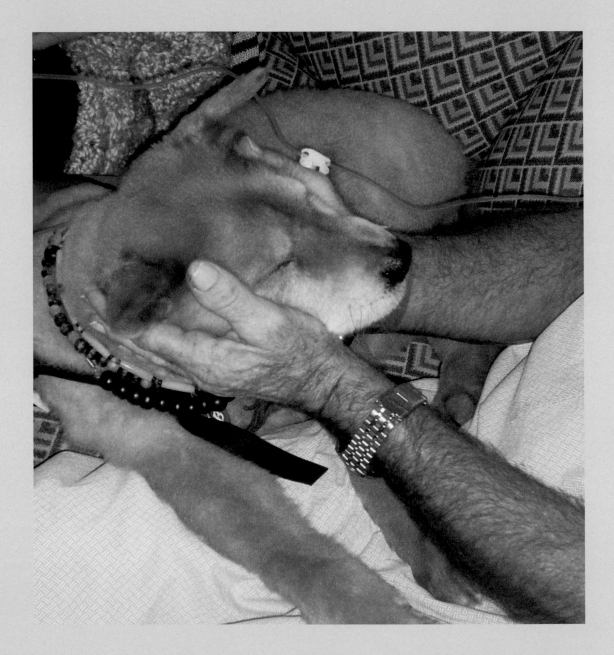

Dennis, Baxter, and I enter the room that almost says, "Welcome all dogs, especially if you're Baxter."

I proceed to place Baxter in bed with our now actively dying patient. They've just taken him to spend some time outdoors. It's an exquisite day, and they thought the fresh air would awaken his soul. Maybe only God and Baxter can do that. The wife, in her wheelchair, gets next to Baxter, who's nestled next to her husband with his arm resting on Baxter's head. She has placed it there, thinking it will make a difference. And it does, both for her and for them. Camera phones start clicking, and each of them wants a photo with the patient. Baxie is the theme, and he poses. All the others line up for the same exact photo. All want to be remembered with their father this way . . . with Baxter.

These are perfect moments . . . perfect moments with their dying spouse, father, friend.

After the photo session, we leave. Fifteen minutes later we are outside on the lovely grounds, visiting with another patient. All of a sudden, the other son taps Dennis on the shoulder.

"Please excuse me." His voice quivers. His face is flushed. "My father just died, and Baxter is a legend in our family. He made such a difference for all of us. He made my dad's death perfect—better, more peaceful, easier to handle. Thank you, thank you so much for being there with Baxter. I can't tell you how grateful I am. I actually feel good. I think that Baxter brought my dad a sense that it was okay to die. And he made it okay for us, too."

You can't question the validity of any of this. Baxter made the family's experience special, more interesting, and less painful. He brought a liveliness to a room full of very sad people and one dying man. He made it all better.

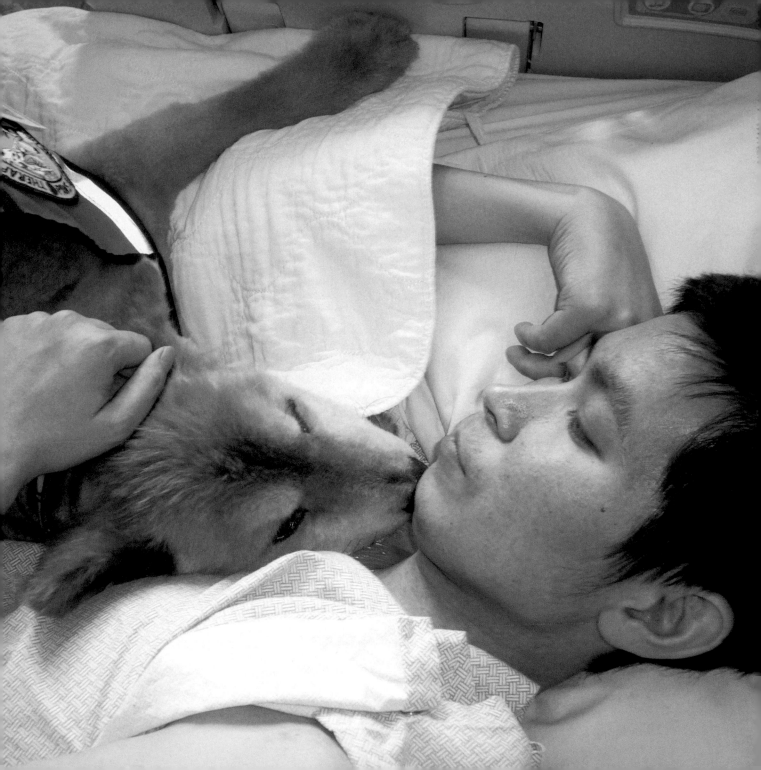

B A X T E R

IS

R E Q U E S T E D

Before I can even get through the side door leading directly to patients' rooms, Thong, a young Vietnamese woman, requests Baxter for her husband, Wee.

In we go with Baxter, where this 31-year-old man is curled up with his pillow, lying on top of the bedspread. His wife now sits in a big armchair brought from home, or recently bought just for her to be comfortable in her husband's room.

She's knitting a lime-green something-or-other and has what looks like a lifetime supply of colored yarns in a see-through bag. This area of the room looks like home for Thong and Wee. Accordingly, she invites Baxter into their world.

The view outside from Wee's room is stunning. Inside, however, sadness rules and pain is the barometer for an array of emotions, from grief to helplessness. Wee pushes the button on his pain pump as I glance over at him.

"Your wife tells me you would like to meet Baxter."

"I think it's my wife who wants to be with Baxter. She loves dogs."

"I see. But wouldn't you want to have Baxter next to you in bed just for a moment, just to see what he might be able to do for you?"

He looks at me incredulously. I can almost hear the voice in his head: *How can a dog offer me solace from this terrible suffering?*

I decide to be a little forthright, to demonstrate the answer to the question I see on his face.

I put Baxter next to Wee, and he doesn't move away; instead he curls up to him the way he would a body pillow. With his special gifts, Baxter senses that this man needs some care and he places his head close to Wee's.

Everyone in the room makes that "oooh" noise. "Isn't he cute? Look at him."

A couple of times Baxter changes his position, but only to move closer to Wee, who embraces the moment by not moving away.

"If at any time you've had enough, just let me know."

"Okay, you can take him away to my wife. She really wants to be with him."

"Thong, why don't you go on the sofa and let Baxter sit next to you. Would that be okay?"

"Sure."

I put Baxie right next to her. As she cuddles with him, he places his head on her leg. She smiles.

"Look, Wee, look how cute he is."

Wee manages to form his lips into an understanding smile. He wants to see his wife happy.

His grandmother is there, too, as well as Thong's mother. Everyone is smiling. Everyone. Finally, this family has a positive distraction: Baxter.

"What about Grandma? Would she like to sit with Baxter?"

"No, she's scared of dogs. In fact, she's never even touched a dog."

Grandma speaks no English, so Thong translates. Grandma smiles. I touch her to encourage her to sit alongside Baxter. After a few minutes, she concedes; Thong

I HOPE THAT OUR TIME HERE, FOR THESE MOMENTS, BRINGS RESPITE FROM THE DARK, EMPTY SPOT THAT IS ON THE HORIZON FOR THONG.

gets up and Grandma sits down. Baxter's head is now on her lap.

And, once more, the whole room is smiling . . . for this moment. Baxter has brought delight and wonder to this family in the midst of woe and dread.

"This is a good day for Wee. He's been sleeping for several days and has been in much pain. I'm so glad that he can enjoy watching Baxter with our family."

As I am leaving, Thong stops me. "Tell me your name," she says.

"Melissa," I reply.

"Thank you, Melissa."

"And pronounce your name for me," I request.

She makes the sound for me. "My name means 'love' in Vietnamese."

I can't help the tears that form in my eyes as I try to understand what she's enduring. I weep for my inadequacy, my struggle to find words that can express my feelings. I know that, incapable of words, Baxter understands more than I do. I hope, though, that our time here, for these moments, brings respite from the dark, empty spot that is on the horizon for Thong.

Kathleen, Wee's nurse, tells me that Thong cries often. This, I can understand.

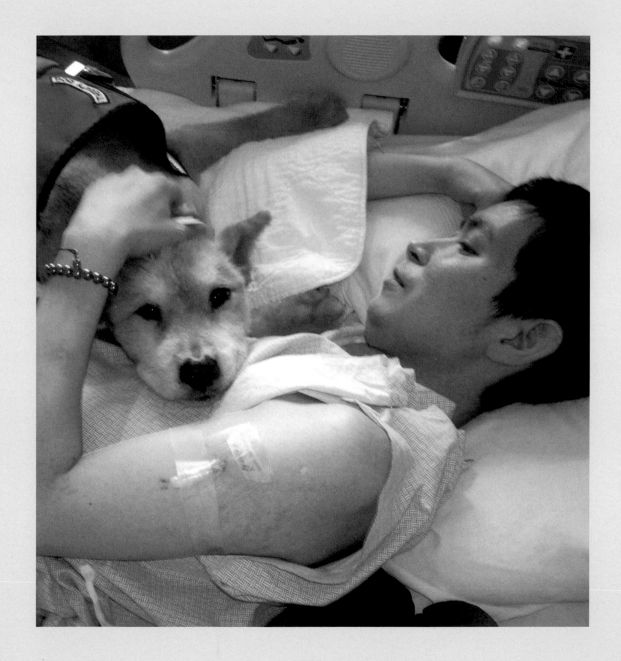

FAMILY

PHOTO

Emily is a devoted granddaughter who was practically reared by her grandmother, Corazón, who is dying. Emily informs me, "*Corazón* means 'heart.'"

Corazón, covered in her handmade red afghan, looks like a porcelain doll. Her lips are coated in a

THEY LOOK HAPPY
AS BAXTER TAKES THEM
TO ANOTHER PLACE ...
FOR A MOMENT ...
FOR A SNAPSHOT OF TIME.

cherry shade. Though Filipino, she looks Chinese.

"You know, Baxter," Emily says, "Cora loved you in bed with her, but she's too close to death for this now. Do you understand?"

Baxter stares at Emily. Their dark eyes meet. This is confirmation to her that Baxter senses what she's saying. "But I need you, Baxter. And my sisters Allison and Angela do, too. And so does my father. We all need you to comfort us."

The sofa bed is covered in their bedspread and pillows, lending a hominess to the room. Someone spends every night with Corazón. A familiar pop song plays on the CD player. It is music that the girls can relate to, not Grandma.

Angela strokes Grandma's forehead. She whispers to her. "Granny, Baxter is here. Baxter came to see you. I love you, Granny."

Angela goes to the sofa, where I place Baxter next to her. He puts his head on her lap. Allison comes over from the chair by her grandmother's bed and sits halfway on the arm of the sofa. The spread is crumpled up under her. She leans into Angela, who says, "Maybe I should just get up so that you can sit by Baxter."

Allison doesn't fight her on this offer. She moves into Angela's place. Angela returns to her grandmother's bedside. Allison leans into Baxter and strokes him for as long as we're there, over an hour. She almost falls asleep with Baxter's body partially on hers. His head hangs off the edge. His paws are curled into the middle of Allison's legs.

Now the father, Emil, reaches over to touch Baxter and talks to him. "I've never met you, but I've heard so much about you from my wife, my mother-in-law, and my daughters."

Emil grabs Baxter's paw and begins to shake it. "It's a real pleasure to finally meet you. Thank you for the comfort you give my family."

He begins telling stories to distract everyone from the sadness. His children learn for the first time that he had long hair in his younger days. Their mouths drop open in unison. "Yeah, it was to my shoulders, but I didn't put it in a ponytail."

They're laughing, making fun of their father.

"When I worked in the pharmacy department I received free samples of Rogaine. When the free samples stopped coming, my hair stopped growing, and then started to just fall out."

Emily, Allison, and Angela are by now laughing hysterically. None of us, though, is oblivious to Cora, whose breathing is interrupted by short coughs. We're respectful of her, but the family is also enjoying this respite. And Baxter's in the middle of the whole show. Emil explains that a framed family photo hangs in the den of their home. It is a family legend that it cost $800. Emil confesses that in the photo, his "hair" was airbrushed on. "But," he adds, "that wasn't why it was so expensive."

Again, everyone laughs, and I can tell it feels good to them. Their shoulders drop along with the heavy burden of imminent loss and sadness. Now, all of them are on the sofa and Baxter is in Allison's lap. "Is he too heavy for you?"

"No," she replies demurely.

"All of you on the sofa world make a lovely family portrait," Dennis says. "I would be happy to capture this moment. I won't charge you $800 either. But I don't provide airbrushing."

They all pose, reaching out to Baxter to pull him in close, to be a part of their family. Dennis captures the family at a time when death is not on their faces but not far from their hearts. They look happy as Baxter takes them to another place . . . for a moment . . . for a snapshot of time. They will remember this moment and the photo . . . all for free.

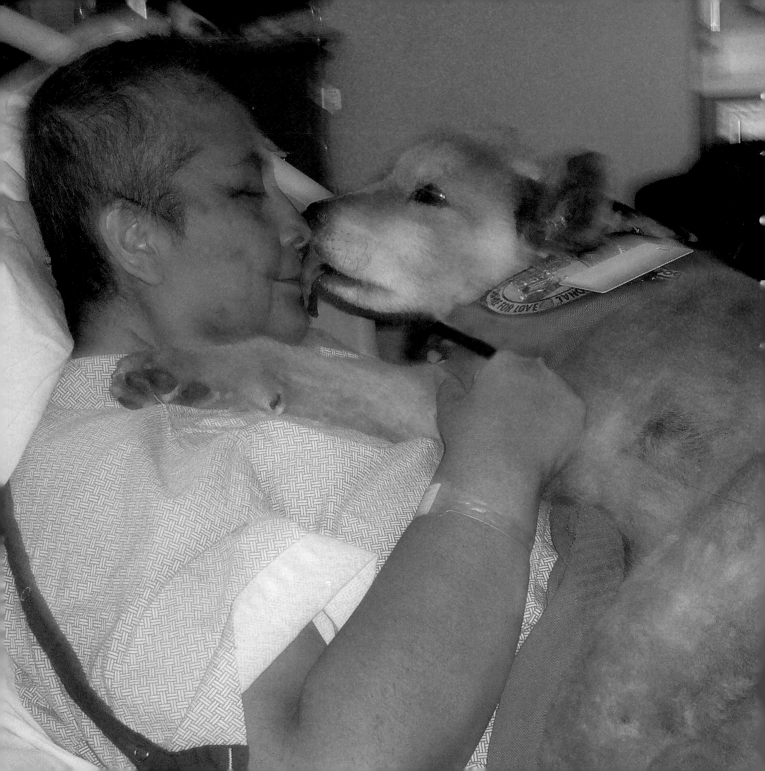

HE'S
AN
ANGEL

I peek in the doorway as I knock on the door. "Hello, we have a little therapy dog. Would you like to see him?"

The patient peeks over the bed, beyond her pillow. Her dark eyes seem to become a shade lighter when she sees Baxter.

"I can put him in bed with you if you would like."

"Oh, that would be great. Put him right here."

I assume there is pain there, because she has a pillow across her stomach.

"Right there? In your lap? He weighs thirty-eight pounds, and that might be uncomfortable for you."

"No, please, put him here."

She points to her pillow.

"Okay. Here goes."

Maria responds with a smile. She wraps her body all around Baxter and speaks to him. "You make me so happy. I'm so happy right now because of you. Before you came in here, I was sad. I was crying. Baxter, why does this have to happen to me? Why do I have to have cancer? Why me? And it's all over my body. I'm forty-five with four children and I have cancer. But I have faith. I believe in God.

"Oh, come here, Baxter. Come closer. Look at these ears. You're like an angel. You have angel ears. I love you. I want to marry you."

Baxter is now looking into her eyes, and she into his. Baxter kisses her, and she continues to hold him like a baby.

"Maria, you have to be okay with polygamy, because Baxter has been asked many times to marry. You can imagine, he's quite a popular guy."

"That's okay. If I can have some moments with him every day, I don't care what happens."

Kathleen, the nurse, enters to change Maria's pain patch.

"I'm busy with Baxter. Can you come back?"

Kathleen is very understanding.

> "BAXTER YOU
> AREN'T A DOG;
> YOU'RE AN ANGEL!"

"If I were in bed with Baxter, I wouldn't want to be bothered either. I'll come back in about fifteen minutes."

Maria exclaims this, after moments with Baxter: "Baxter you aren't a dog; you're an angel!"

Baxter stays with her for some time until the phone rings. I take him away from her arms. Maria waves good-bye, and we hear Baxter's name and "angel" mentioned in the telephone conversation.

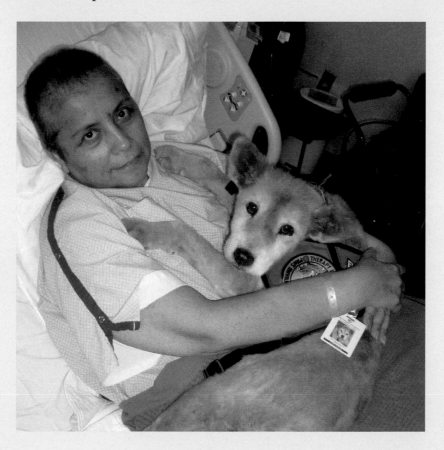

COME HERE,

BAXTER

Donald greets Baxter in the hallway as he's making his way back to his room. He's young and handsome in his hiking boots. One hand holds onto a pole on wheels that carries the pain medication flowing into his veins. Though dying, Donald continues to keep himself moving.

"Oh, who is this? What a precious dog!"

Donald bends down on his knees to meet Baxter face to face. He begins petting him.

"This is Baxter, a therapy dog."

"Oh, I love him. I just love him!" He continues to rub Baxter down and make a fuss over him.

"I can bring him to your room if you would like. What room are you in?"

"104, just right over there." He tilts his head to indicate the direction.

I push open the door for him. The room is dark. The blinds are closed to the lovely day outside. There's nothing that seems to be lovely in Donald's life today except for Baxter.

"Come here, boy."

I pick up Baxter and put him on a bedspread I've laid over the sofa right next to Donald. Immediately, he has his hands all over Baxter. He leans his head against Baxter's.

I introduce Dennis. "This is my husband, Dennis." Donald extends his hand.

"Hello, sir. It's nice to meet you."

"Dennis is in charge of the music here. Would you like him to get some music for your room?"

He names some meditation-type group, but I don't recognize the name.

> ONLY BAXTER AND LOVE ARE IN BETWEEN DONALD AND ME. WE HUG FOR MANY MOMENTS. I'M NOT SURE WHAT I'M FEELING, BUT I KNOW IT'S SOMETHING SPECIAL. WE'RE BOTH GRATEFUL FOR THIS MOMENT.

"I know we don't have that, but we do have some other types of meditation music."

Dennis leaves and brings back some possibilities for Donald, trying to satisfy his desire.

I remain with him as he has a private conversation with Baxter. Baxter transforms the dull ambiance of the room to one of warmth.

"Have you had any other therapy dogs visit you?"

"I don't need another therapy dog. I just need Baxter."

The light barely inches in from the gorgeous afternoon as the accordion blinds flicker back and forth from the tepid air that emanates from the overhead vents. It's very warm in Donald's room. I remove my jacket.

"Are you warm?" Donald asks me.

"Oh, maybe it's just a hot flash. This is part of turning fifty."

"You're lucky. I'll never reach that age."

"I'm so sorry."

"I have full-blown colon cancer and there's nothing they can do."

All the while, he continues to love on Baxter and each time he strokes him, he smiles.

Dennis returns with just the right CD, though it's not what Donald really wanted. He shows the cover to Donald.

"Yeah, that looks good."

"May I put it on now?"

"Yes, please. That sounds lovely."

I want to make sure that we're not over-staying our welcome. "Are you in any pain?"

"No. Yesterday I was really bad, but today I feel so much better."

"I'm so glad to hear that. Are you feeling tired?"

"No, I'm just getting comfortable." He readjusts himself on the sofa.

"May I get you another pillow?"

"No, all I need is Baxter. He brings me such comfort."

Donald holds him hard like a teddy bear.

"He's such a beautiful dog."

"Thank you. I think so, too. Can I get you anything before we leave?"

"No thank you. Thank you so much for coming and bringing Baxter."

"We'll leave you a small collection of New Age music that I think you might like."

He looks over at me, extending his arms for a hug. I move toward him. Only Baxter and love are in between Donald and me. We hug for many moments. I'm not sure what I'm feeling, but I know it's something special. We're both grateful for this moment.

Then, he extends his hand to Dennis and they shake.

"Good-bye, Donald."

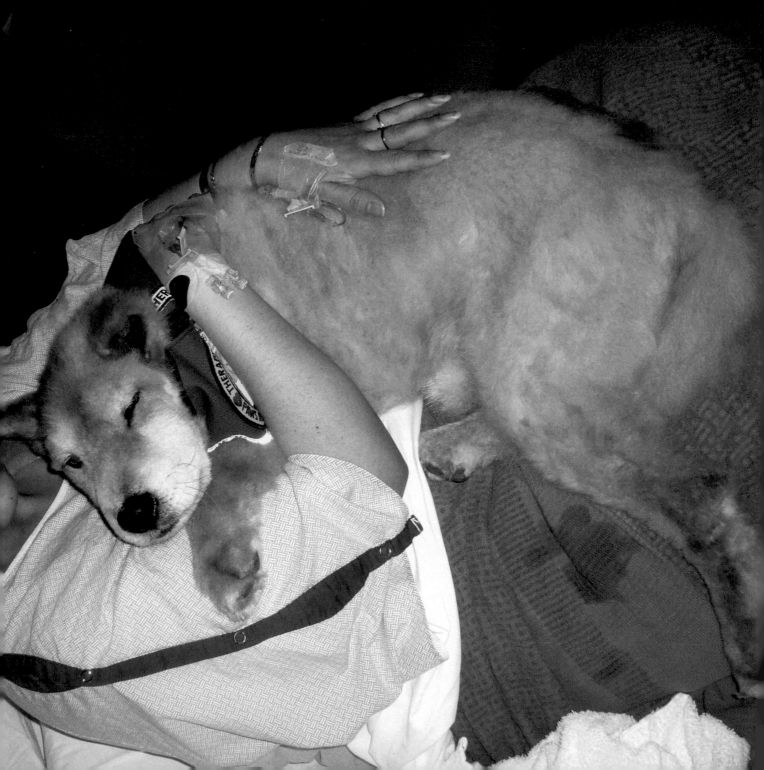

THE IMPRINT

OF AN

ANGEL

Two women who look like sisters are admiring Baxter, who is ahead of me in the hallway. As they speak to him, one of the nurses points to me. "She's the owner."

"Hello," I say.

"Could you please take Baxter in to see Sally?" one of the women asks. "She loves dogs and I think she would really like to meet Baxter."

"Absolutely," I reply.

Baxter follows me into the room at his snail's pace, inching along. He's in no hurry, though the family members seem in a hurry for him to meet Sally.

Sally is thirty-seven, and she's wearing her own pajamas instead of the hospice gown. Her bed is at an angle so that it faces the parklike setting outside her large windows and French doors.

"Hello, Sally. I hear that you like dogs. Would you like for Baxter to lie beside you in your bed?"

She nods her head and I proceed to place him in the small space next to her. Immediately, she smiles and pets Baxter. He responds by moving his face so he can lick her hands.

"Do you mind that he is licking you?"

"No, I really like it."

"He's so cute," one of the sisters says. "What is he?"

"He's an angel of sorts. He's part golden retriever and part chow."

"I've never seen a dog that looks this way."

Members of the family seem to be pleased that Sally is captivated by Baxter. This arrangement doesn't last too long, because it's dinner time and Sally eagerly looks forward to the meals at hospice.

"I'm having my favorite tonight: a grilled cheese sandwich."

I know this is a cue for me to move Baxter. I slide Sally's tray table across her bed and attempt to assist her.

"I can do that. I'm used to this," claims Sally's mother.

Her mother is a lovely woman with a put-together, attractive presentation. She smiles at me.

There's a tension in the room and I want to relieve it in some way.

"How about if I move Baxter on the sofa in between you and your sister after you finish assisting your daughter?"

The mom's expression changes from over-whelmed and uneasy to relaxed and relieved. She perks up right away at the thought that she is going to get a breather . . . she's going to get some time away from her emotional pain and unburden her-self on Baxter. "Okay then."

Her sister, too, is there awaiting Baxter. They both want him. Each extends her arms, vying for a position of closeness to Baxter, as I walk toward the sofa with him in my arms. I place him in between them.

WHEN WE LEAVE, I CAN SEE WHERE BAXTER WAS IN SALLY'S BED. I SEE THE IMPRINT OF AN ANGEL.

With his paws on one and his head on the other, he connects with them, easing their sadness, offering them a respite from Sally's complex condi-tion. For these moments, enough bliss exists to create some inner healing. It's a moment for Sally's mom and aunt to catch their breaths, to get some therapy for themselves.

"He's so soft," murmurs Sally's aunt.

"What a face!" Sally's mom declares. "This is the most irresistible dog that I've ever seen. We've always had dogs. I will never be without a dog in my home. But this dog is something special. He's unusual. He has something about him that just grabs me and pulls me in to him, pulls me away from my grief. He calms the spirit."

"How many years apart are you and your sister?" I ask.

"Just two years, and we're very close."

"That's wonderful that you can be here for each other."

Her sister, Sally's aunt, tears up.

"I had a dog for fourteen years. I loved him so much and it was too sad when he died. I've not had another dog since. It feels so good to touch Baxter. It's soothing."

Dennis comes in with some suggestions for music. "How about some nice music for you, Sally?"

"I would like that." She just needs some soft background music, her mother adds. Dennis returns with some selections.

"I like that. That's really nice. Thank you," Sally tells Dennis.

Baxter visits with the sisters for some time and we discover that we're practically neighbors of Sally's aunt and uncle.

"It's been a pleasure meeting all of you. I'm so glad that you asked Baxter to come meet Sally. And now I'm glad that everyone got to be with Baxter."

"Baxter's happy being with all of you. I'm sure we'll see you again, Sally. We'll be back in two days and we'll check on you. Maybe you will want Baxter in bed with you again."

"That would be very nice of you. Thank you, Baxter, for coming by."

TWO DAYS LATER

We enter Sally's room, where she's now dressed in red pajamas. Her bed is still angled at the lovely outdoor setting where she can see squirrels, rabbits, birds, and lots of periwinkles and pure white agapanthus in full bloom. Soon, those perfect flowers will fade away and someone else will be in Sally's room. What a profound contrast, or is it just the inevitable cycle of life and death?

"Hello, Sally. We told you we would be back. How about having Baxter again in bed next to you?"

"That would be great."

She inches over and I place Baxter beside her. She seems more available on this visit, not as tired.

Baxter can tell that she wants to love on him. Again, he licks her, but this time when he stops, Sally methodically rubs his face all around his muzzle.

"Sally, did you know that you have the only room with a hummingbird feeder outside? Oh, look, there it is, and there's a hummingbird there right now. How special is that!"

Sally's caregiver enters. "Hello, I'm Patricia. I've been with Sally for about a year now."

"She's family," says Sally.

That told me all I needed to know of the depth and profundity of Patricia and Sally's relationship.

As Baxter rests in Sally's hands, I see that he's oblivious to anything around him. His eyes are on Sally.

"I'd like to get Baxter a little closer to you so that you can get the teddy bear feel from him."

I get a pillow and place it on Sally's lap.

"If at any point you're uncomfortable with this, just let me know. I don't want to hurt you. How's your belly?"

"It's fine."

I place Baxter on top of Sally's lap and she cuddles with him. "He feels like a baby. This is wonderful."

Patricia puts it all in perspective. "We do have bad days, but Sally and I try to turn that all around."

"I think this is what Baxter teaches me," I respond. "It's all about moments and living in the moment. And to have a sense of humor. He never lets anything get to him. He moves through it to the other side right away, always staying in the present. He doesn't hold a grudge, because that would keep him back there rather than right here. He teaches me to forgive."

"Sally is not quick to let people into her life. It's only when she really likes someone that she allows them to get close to her." Patricia freely divulges this information about Sally.

Sally looks at me, then looks at Baxter. Her look says it all. She's beaming, holding onto Baxter. Sally has a great laugh and a big smile. She has a fantastic sense of humor, too. We laugh a lot as Sally demonstrates over and over again her affection for Baxter. She looks like she is at the beginning of her life, a mere child having a moment with her stuffed animal. Instead, she's a young woman at the end of her life.

"Baxter is the epitome of 'actions speak louder than words,' " I say. "And he's coming in loud and clear with you, Sally. Can you hear him? Can you feel his love?"

"I can, and it makes me feel full."

Baxter decides to change positions. He wants off the pillow and next to Sally. He wants her to hold his face in her hand and rub his muzzle.

Sally begins to talk directly to Baxter. "You have a cold, wet nose, don't you? I'll warm it up for you. I just love your ears. It's not that I don't like your face. But those ears! They're special."

"I tell people that he has big ears because he's an angel and his ears are his wings," I reply.

Patricia can't let that one go. "Sally's an angel, too."

"I believe that Baxter, on some level, senses that."

When we leave, I can see where he was in Sally's bed. I see the imprint of an angel.

"Baxter wishes you well when you go home next week." I tell her this as we walk out the door.

Patricia and Sally echo simultaneously, "Bye, Baxter."

BETWEEN A CHILD
AND
A SAGE

Erin is one of the acupuncture and massage team leaders who service hospice. As part of the volunteer staff, Baxter qualifies for this service. At almost eighteen, he longs for such remedies for his aching joints and other inflamed appendages. Everyone notices his arthritis when he limps from room to room, and especially when he struggles to get up from a prone position. He makes each step with extreme effort, and his lying down is more like falling down; his getting up will make you wince.

Baxter, though, is stoic. He's a wonderful mentor for me for how to live life. He teaches me invaluable lessons by his actions. Here's some of what Baxter has taught me:

- Don't complain about your ailments, and be open to all sorts of remedies even if you think they're weird.

- Don't react to others when you're feeling bad. Just continue to give love, and that will attract love into your life.

- Be brave, strong, and confident. Go through life with a loving spirit. This is more powerful than any weapon like biting, growling, whining, or fighting.

- Get excited about eating. Strut to the food bowl. Don't overeat, but eat until you're full because you're not going to eat again for several hours. This is another reason not to be picky.

- Drink lots of water, preferably with ice. Ignore what the dentists say. Eat those ice chips. They cool you off when it's warm outside.

- Find a bed to sleep in, preferably one that has someone in it. You need to have someone to cuddle. You don't want to spend too much time alone.

Many different people work on Baxter. He's the first dog any of them has ever "needled," though no one seems fearful of making a design of needles in places that correspond to areas like his gallbladder. Erin will say, "Put one in gallbladder 7."

Baxter has no idea what they're saying, but he remains calm, lying on his side while four trained interns give him some relief so that he can better perform his job.

Baxter looks up at me while all this is happening. His eyes tell all.

"Okay, Mom. I know these needles are going to help me. They hurt, but I'll remain strong and go along with this. It isn't that bad. Anyway, I do love all the fuss and attention. Look at all these women hovering over me. I'm the center of their lives for these moments."

With the needles in, Margi begins to do Reiki on him, touching him in special ways, gingerly moving tender fingers up and down to massage his spine, which protrudes visibly through his bald spots. He completely luxuriates in all the attention, the baby talk, and, of course, the touch. There are occasions when one of them takes that needle to a sensitive place, a hard spot, which causes him to turn his head and roll his eyes such that a little portion of the white shows. Then, he proceeds to lick the practitioner's hand and lie back down.

> "BAXTER KNOWS ABOUT DEATH AND DYING BECAUSE IT'S ORGANIC FOR DOGS. IT'S PART OF THEIR EXISTENCE AND THEY ACCEPT IT; THEY DON'T FIGHT IT. THEY LIVE ONE MOMENT AT A TIME."

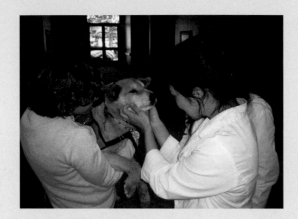

No one expects that Baxie will growl or nip or bite, even when someone jars a painful place. There's trust in Baxter that he will always remain in therapy mode, never reacting, responding, or demanding. This trust enables the healers to do their work without fear.

Frequently, they will all be gathered in their official white coats. When Baxter enters, all eyes immediately turn to him. Each of them has a special, individual connection to Baxter. One by one, they get down on their knees and make contact, sometimes literally lying on the floor face to face to get some therapy for themselves.

It's an exchange. They work on him and he "works" on them. It's a meeting of the hearts. I ask Erin what it is about Baxie that makes him so special to her, to her team.

"He's like a child, so full of sweetness, yet at the same time, a sage. I see what he knows—he knows about death and dying because it's organic for dogs, for animals. It's part of their existence and they accept it; they don't fight it. They aren't preoccupied with it, coating it with euphemisms. They live one moment at a time."

"Wow, Erin. I really like what you said. Look at Baxter. I think he's smiling at you."

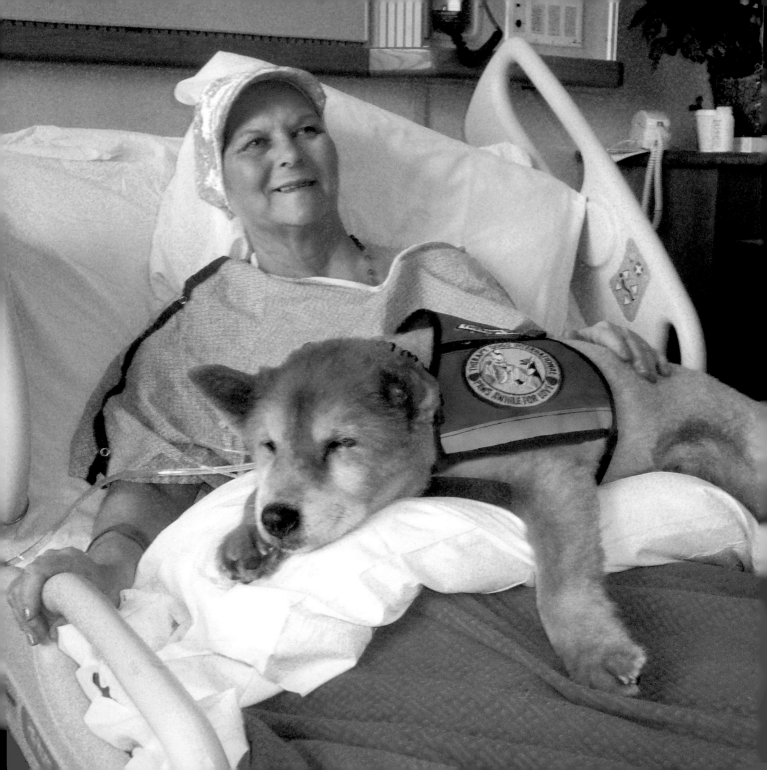

BEST FRIENDS

FOR

LIFE

Sue and Patti have been best friends since they were little girls. Now adults, Patti rarely leaves Sue's side as she lays dying. Jim, Sue's husband, gives them plenty of room to carry on. He remains laconic, the complete antithesis of Patti, who animates the continuous stream of stories from their childhood.

SMILES REPLACE FROWNS,
JOY REPLACES SORROW,
PEACE REPLACES FEAR,
AND WELL-BEING
REPLACES PAIN.
IT'S MAGICAL.

Jim is not jealous. He's too full of sadness for that. He appreciates their need to hold on to a time when things were different.

Sue can barely talk. She mumbles words here and there, but basically it's Patti reliving their friendship for her. Patti acts out everything for Sue. "Remember when you had that dog who loved to roll in the grass?" Patti says, and she goes to the floor and wiggles like a puppy. They laugh and cry, hug and kiss, telling each other good-bye through their memories, which will live on just like this moment.

As close as Sue and Patti are, and as long and warm as the marriage is between Sue and Jim, there's room for Baxter. He comes in between and all around them. He never interrupts their stories, their silent moments, their tears and laughter. Instead, Baxter adds to everyone's moments, bringing a softness, a love, an innocence that cannot be matched. He's there for all three of them, but it's Sue who finds Baxter to be like a tranquilizer, calming her anxiety, kissing her wounds, identifying with her pain, and sharing his endless love.

Sue loves animals . . . all animals. She lives on a farm and adores every living creature, from squirrels to pigs. Baxter knows this. As he curls up to Sue the grimace on her face grows softer, smoother, more peaceful. It's what I call a "Baxter Moment." It's a perfect scene where Baxter eviscerates everything bad and love is all there is. Smiles replace frowns, joy replaces sorrow, peace replaces fear, and well-being replaces pain. It's magical.

Patti and Jim will tell you so.

When Baxter comes to visit Sue, everything bad disappears and everything good replaces it.

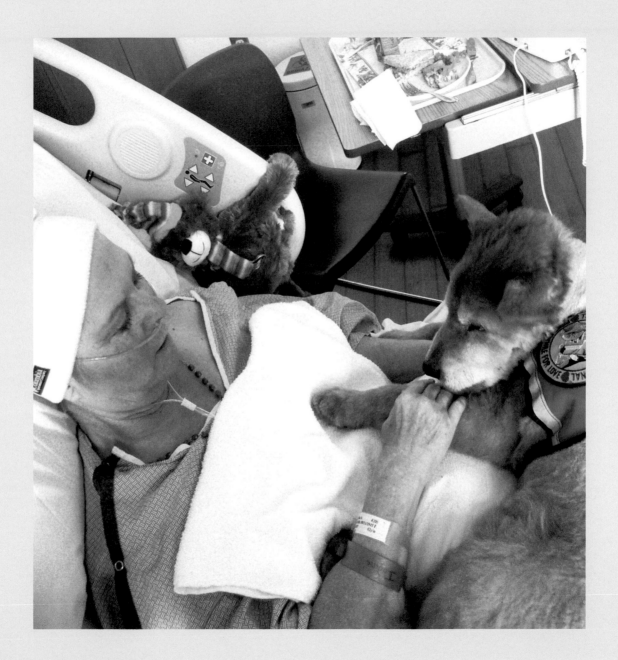

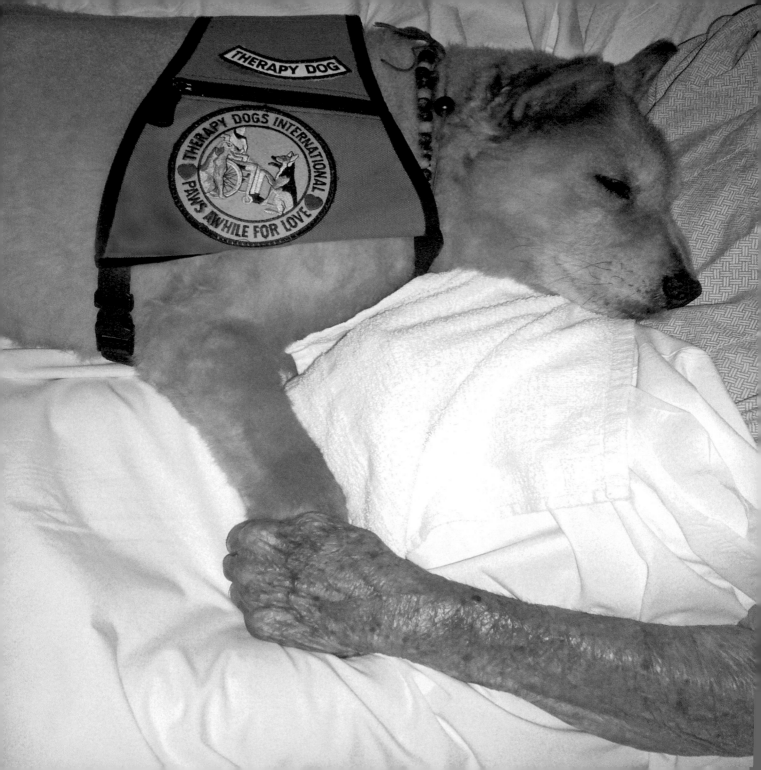

GREEK

GIRLS

Baxter is a showstopper. He enters hospice and takes his position on the floor near the common area. Three young women approach him as if they are meeting Brad Pitt for the first time. Their jaws drop in unison. What ensues is tantamount to a request for Baxter's autograph.

THE FAMILY MEMBERS SPEAK GREEK TO EACH OTHER. I DON'T UNDERSTAND, BUT BAXTER IS MULTILINGUAL. HE KNOWS THEY'RE TALKING ABOUT HIM. WHEN HE HEARS HIS NAME MENTIONED, HE WAGS HIS TAIL.

"Oh, look how cute!"

"Look at him. Couldn't you just eat him up?"

"Yes, in one bite."

"Here's his business card," I say.

"Oh, he is an angel! He's so soft. Feel him."

"Maybe you can go see my father. My father loves dogs."

After all this, Baxter gets up and follows them. We check in on their father, but he is sleeping, so we leave. They continue to indulge Baxter with their loving expressions.

One of the women gets on the floor with Baxter and just stares at him. "I just love this little dog. He's so precious." I sit with her for a while.

Barbara, a nurse, reaches down to rub Baxter, sharing a place with this young woman. "All of us here, we love Baxter. When we see him coming, we all start smiling. We really get a kick out of him. You should see him when he gets in bed with the patients. It's amazing."

As Barbara endorses all the wonders of Baxter, this young woman is even more smitten. Now, the whole family approaches Baxter. His presence is contagious. You can't see him and not touch him.

We try again to see the patient. As we enter the room, the patient smiles as soon as he sees Baxter. I can see that moving him over so Baxter can get in bed with him would be an impossible feat, so I grab the most comfortable chair in the room and place Baxter there, facing the patient.

The exchanges that occur among the family members are all in Greek. I don't understand them, but Baxter is multilingual. He knows they're talking about him. His ears are perky and his eyes wide. When he hears his name mentioned, he wags his tail. All eyes are on him.

Michele, the patient's nurse, enters to administer a pill. Before she leaves, she stops to hug Baxter.

A few minutes later, the patient throws up.

Baxter is totally calm. His head is hanging off the chair onto the pillow that rests under the patient's arm. The girls are spraying rosewater to mitigate the unpleasant odor. Baxter remains there for the patient. As the wife freshens up her husband, I get cool washcloths for his forehead. No one disputes my gesture.

I suggest ice chips for his nausea. The patient takes some and begins to feel better.

Baxter loves ice chips. I take the spoon and put a few chips in my hand. I hold out my hand for Baxter to take the chips. "See, he likes them, too."

Baxter chomps away in chorus with the patient. For these few moments, the emotional pain subsides and one of the daughters laughs out loud.

"Tell us about the badge on Baxter's uniform."

"It's an indication that he is certified to be a therapy dog. He passed the test issued by Therapy Dogs International, administered by a certification officer."

They translate for the patient. His eyes shut. The wife says, "I think my husband would like to go to sleep now."

I grab Baxter and he bids them all farewell with his signature look.

One of the daughters follows him out and hugs me. "I'm so glad that I got to meet Baxter. He's just wonderful."

BARRY'S

NURSE

Barry's nurse, Michele, requests that Baxter visit Barry in room 105.

"Barry is quite disfigured. I've never seen anyone with this disease, Neurofibromatosis Type I. He's a wonderful person and I believe Baxter can make a difference."

A few moments later, a small, elderly woman with a bent-over frame approaches us in the hallway.

"Are you going to take the dog to see Barry? I've been a friend of Barry's for over thirty years. I know Barry and I believe he would love to meet such an adorable dog."

"Yes, Barry's nurse, Michele, already told us about your friend."

The three of us enter Barry's room. Country music is blaring from the CD player. All at once, my ears stop hearing the music. I'm overwhelmed and startled by the figure in the wheelchair. A voice comes to me.

You don't have to do this. You can leave. You have a choice.

As these selfish words play over and over in my head, I am brought to my senses. Really I am humbled . . . by Baxter. He goes right up to Barry's wheelchair and begins licking Barry's leg, and then the arm that hangs down from the wheelchair seeking to touch Baxter.

If he can do it, then I can do it, too.

I realize that Baxter doesn't see what I see. He sees only what matters . . . the character of the individual. All Baxter concerns himself with is giving and receiving love.

> BAXTER DOESN'T SEE WHAT I SEE. HE SEES ONLY WHAT MATTERS ... THE CHARACTER OF THE INDIVIDUAL. ALL BAXTER CONCERNS HIMSELF WITH IS GIVING AND RECEIVING LOVE.

"Hello, Barry. I see that Baxter has already introduced himself to you. I hope you're okay with his licking you like that."

He nods his head.

There's a softness to Barry's eyes and his composure, and now all I can see is what Baxter has shown me. I overlook the features and move toward the inside, toward the character. I want to have Baxter's perspective. I want to experience Barry without passing judgment.

I situate Baxter in a chair, and he responds by giving Barry his paw and then a kiss on Barry's arm. Barry is all over Baxter, as much as he can be in a wheelchair. He strokes Baxter, who responds with kisses and dreamy eye expressions that speak to

Barry. They look at each other with eyes that say, "I love you."

Barry holds Baxter firmly and doesn't seem to want to let go. He's like a soldier clutching his loved one before departing again to war. I am sure Barry, with this grave affliction, has fought many wars in his fifty years on the planet.

Baxter gives Barry unconditional love. And Baxter teaches me an invaluable lesson about love.

"Barry, if you were in your bed or on the sofa, you could be even closer to Baxter. Then you could cuddle with him."

Barry turns his head to look at the sofa.

"Would you like to lie down now and have Baxter next to you?"

He nods.

"I'll go get Michele to move you."

Michele enters and takes Barry's feet from the wheelchair platforms.

"Looks like your edema has receded."

Barry doesn't respond.

Michele helps him up and tries to get him comfortable on the sofa. She puts pillows around him, and then I place Baxter beside Barry.

He lowers his body and his head to have it against Baxter's face. Baxter kisses him. Barry hugs Baxter. His arms are completely surrounding Baxter's neck. Baxter lays his head on Barry's lap.

Michele was right. Baxter does make it all better for Barry for these moments.

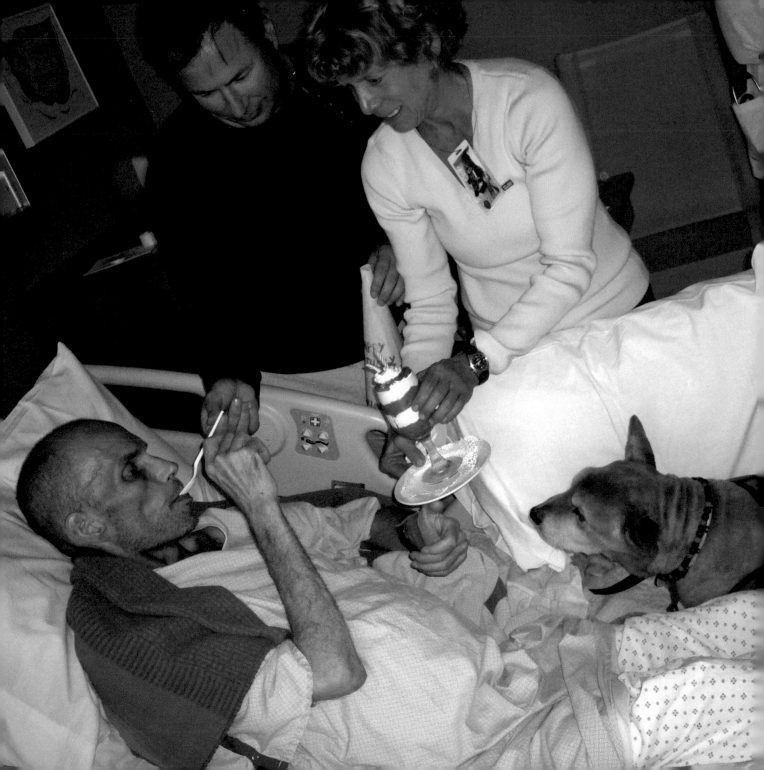

DONALD'S
BIRTHDAY

When we arrive at hospice, one of the nurses informs us that today is Donald's birthday. He is forty-four, and this birthday will be his last.

"Let's make a birthday hat for Baxter and take him to see Donald," I suggest.

We get some construction paper and roll it into a

cone. We then thread a tourniquet strap through the makeshift hat and affix it around Baxter's head. Nothing seems to faze Baxter. He's completely comfortable wearing this hat.

"Off we go, Baxter."

We enter Donald's room, whispering, "Happy birthday." Donald is resting and I place Baxter by his side. He opens his eyes and smiles.

"Baxter wants to wish you a happy birthday, Donald. Check out his hat."

"Happy birthday" seems so sad and useless. I bring him the gift of Baxter's love for his birthday. This seems significant, tangible, and real. The staff, too, play a role in acknowledging Donald's birthday. They are professionals, and they have a way to take this awkward moment and turn it into a moment of kindness.

> "THANK YOU, THANK YOU ALL FOR BEING HERE." DONALD TURNS TO BAXTER. "THANK YOU, BAXTER, FOR LOVING ME."

"I see Baxter came to help you celebrate your birthday."

Both chaplains are present, five nurses, and the aromatherapist, Rodney, who brings the "birthday cake."

The food service staff has made a dessert that Donald requested for his birthday: a pumpkin swirl something-or-other in a parfait glass.

We all sing "Happy Birthday" as Baxter lies in Donald's arms. It is a very bittersweet moment.

"Thank you, thank you all for being here." Donald turns to Baxter. "Thank you, Baxter, for loving me."

"Would you like to taste this?" I ask.

He nods. I spoon some of the dessert into his mouth and I can tell he is having a moment of bliss. The parfait and Baxter just hit the spot. Donald's eyes beam and he smiles.

"Would you like some more?"

He nods faster and harder this time, opening his mouth expressively. He takes several more bites.

"Oh, it is so good. Pass it around the room."

"No, that's okay, Donald. It's all for you. This is your day."

He dozes off, and as Dennis and I leave with Baxter, I contemplate how I would feel lying there knowing forty-four is the oldest I am ever going to be.

INTELLIGENT

BUMP

Verl and Baxter have much in common. For one thing, they are close in age. Verl is ninety-three; Baxter is ninety-six. This puts them in a special category. As Verl says to Baxter, "When the first number in your age is a nine, your time is very, very limited, no matter what. There is no future. There are only moments."

Verl and Baxter live in the moment. They have a trove of both sparkling and dull memories, which carry both of them to this venerable place in life. They have wisdom.

Not everyone is fortunate enough to have wisdom. Baxter has what veterinarians call "an intelligent bump." There is a place on his head that protrudes, which comes after years on the planet.

"I have this bump on the side of my head." Verl leans over to show me a spot that is quite visible through her thinning strands of black and white hair. "Does this count? I earned my wisdom through the school of hard knocks." Then she adds, "But Baxter got lucky. He found you."

And now Baxter and I have found you, Verl. We love that you are able to talk about your life in a joyful manner, without self-pity. You embrace your death like

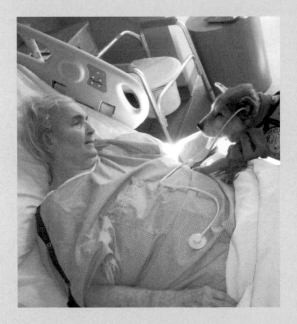

you embrace Baxter. You let go and feel love . . . love for your life and love for Baxter. For this moment, they are the same.

Verl continues: "I was taunted early on in life because I was obese. At the age of thirteen, I dropped out of school and became a maid. I lived with some wonderful families who treated me like family. Over the years, these people became my friends. I had thirty years of a terrible life, thirty years of a wonderful life, and now I'm going out in a blaze of glory."

"Verl, that only makes sixty. What about the other thirty years?"

"Well, that's another story for another time. Now I can say that I've gotten important by being here with the famous Baxter. Two years ago, I was wondering how this would all work out. I knew I was dying and I had no idea where I would go and what I would do. Now look at me. I'm in this wonderful place with loving, helpful people all around me."

"And let's not forget Baxter. He's like some magical wand. He enters, sprinkles his love over the patients, and disappears, but his love remains. He is love. How special is that?"

Like Baxter, Verl has captured the heart of the entire staff at hospice. While we're there, Roger, a nurse, and Holly, a counselor, come by just to say hello and see Baxter with Verl. Baxter and Verl are the stars at the top of the Christmas tree on this, Christmas Day at San Diego Hopsice and The Institute for Palliative Medicine. Though Verl

> THERE'S NO GLOOM AND DOOM IN VERL AND BAXTER'S PRESENCE. I CAN ONLY HOPE THAT I WILL BE LIKE VERL AND BAXTER WHEN I REACH THE END OF MY LIFE.

and Baxter express their wisdom differently, Baxter in his silence and Verl in her didactic stories, each knows they are in a similar place. They are both old, frail, and near the end. This enhances their bond.

Today, Baxter suffers from an ulcerated cornea. His eyelid quivers with pain. Verl can relate to suffering. "I had a terrible morning. My bowels are giving me fits. I was in such discomfort. Oh, Baxter, I'm so sorry that you hurt."

As she talks, she strokes him. I watch her hand as it makes this nonstop up-and-down on Baxter. When you touch Baxter, he touches you back. It's a phenomenon of sorts, inexplicable but practically palpable. The result is that you feel remarkably better . . . for the moment.

"You must have a sense of humor. It's the only way to go through life. I want to make sure that I always know that I'm alive. I don't want to be alive and not know it. That's a burden on everyone else and I don't want to take life away from others.

"I have the end all planned. I told the woman at the mortuary that all I want is the 'toast and toss' treatment. I would like for there to be a headstone that says, 'I told you I was sick.'"

We all laugh. There's no gloom and doom in Verl and Baxter's presence. We listen for every syllable she speaks. We know all of her words count and all that she says is profound. She speaks of politics, religion, and her family of friends as she holds Baxter in her arms. I can only hope that I will be like Verl and Baxter when I reach the end of my life.

A visitor arrives to share the delicious holiday meal prepared by hospice for the patients, which today is free for all visitors, staff, and volunteers. It's a bountiful day in Verl's room, and we leave full before we've had the first bite of turkey.

VERL BECAME LIKE FAMILY AS BAXTER, DENNIS, AND I CONTINUED TO SEE HER OVER THE NEXT SEVERAL WEEKS. I FOUND MYSELF BECOMING ATTACHED TO HER, AS I WAS MOVED BY HER STORY. AS A RESULT, I WANTED TO SHARE WITH HER, BEFORE SHE DIED, THE MOMENTS SHE GAVE TO ME.

I READ THIS STORY TO HER. HER FACE FELL TO HER OUTSTRETCHED HANDS. WHEN SHE LOOKED UP, HER HANDS WERE A BOWL OF TEARS AND HER EYES WERE DRIED UP AND RED. "I ALWAYS WANTED SOMEONE TO KNOW MY STORY. AND NOW YOU'VE CAPTURED A PIECE OF MY LIFE. I DON'T KNOW HOW TO THANK YOU."

I ROSE AND WALKED TOWARD HER WHEELCHAIR. I LEANED OVER AND EMBRACED HER, KNOWING THAT BAXTER HELPED ME TO CREATE THIS STORY.

TOE-LICKING
THERAPY

On occasion, Baxter will choose a room to enter. He'll just head towards the door, walk in, and introduce himself. Though this is obviously not according to protocol, I allow him to do this. He has such a following among the staff at the In-Patient Care Center, that no one has ever complained about his choices.

Having faith in his decision, I always follow him. Today, is one of these days. I watch as he enters with such confidence and clarity that no one could possibly reject him. His head is high, his ears are perky, and his gait has a little bit of an ego to it. Luckily, he is greeted with open arms by both the patient and the family member.

I'M THINKING TO MYSELF THAT THIS JUST DOESN'T SEEM LIKE DEATH. THIS SEEMS LIKE A FUNNY DAY LIVING LIFE.

"Hello," I say. "Baxter has chosen to visit you today. I hope this is a good time for you. Typically, I pick him up and put him in bed with the patient or on the sofa with a friend or family member. I can do either if you would like. It's whatever you prefer."

"I would love for you to put Baxter in bed with me. He can fit right between my feet at the bottom of the bed if that's okay with him."

"But, mom, you won't be able to pet him down there."

"He will be fine right there, honey."

I place Baxter in the only available space and he seems fine. Both mother and daughter are enamored by how cute he is.

"Look at him. He's adorable. Look at that face. What kind of dog is he?" the patient inquires.

"Well, right now, he's a toe licker and this is toe-licking therapy."

Mother and daughter laugh out loud as Baxter helps himself to the mom's toes, and then her whole foot, making his way up her leg.

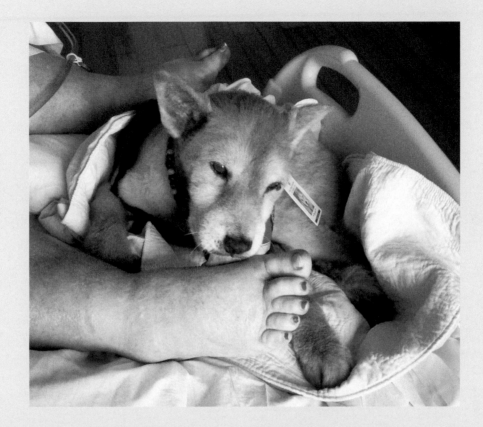

"Oh, that feels so good. I don't get it this good when I have my pedicure."

Again laughter anoints the room, replacing any sort of tears that were previously shared between mom and daughter. Dennis excuses himself to round up a group of nurses to check out the new therapy offered at the In-Patient Care Center.

Baxter has not only brought joy to this family but also to the staff. They are all getting a kick out of Baxter's loving behavior. "This is wonderful. Can I be next?" says one of the nurses.

As Baxter finishes with one foot, I turn him around for the other.

"You know, we have to balance out this toe-licking thing."

The patient smiles and is totally into the craziness of all this. She fans herself and shouts out something just as funny.

"Everytime I do this, I get ten points for exercising my arm. My doctors says that I need to move my upper body as much as I can. Just as toe licking is a new therapy, fanning is a new exercise."

I am sure that you can hear us laughing all the way down the hall. Not one of the staff members, though, asks us to tone it down. In fact, they are making the most noise.

"You should switch arms and get more points and balance that exercise," I say.

Again, we all grin.

I'm thinking to myself that this just doesn't seem like death. This seems like a funny day living life.

Baxter continues, then puts his face underneath her gown kind of by her knees.

"Hey, Baxter, she says, you can go a little further."

"He's very experienced, you know. He's about 95 and really knows what he's doing."

"Well, I'm glad about that. I'll just keep getting exercise points." She fans herself even harder.

By now, we're all hysterical.

As we say our good-byes, I'm amazed again at how my little dog can bring such joy to a group of people, even though one of them is dying.

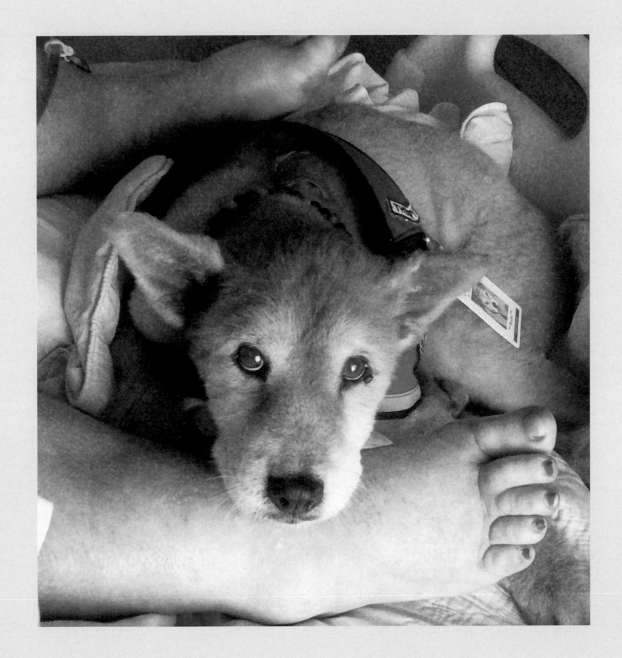

THREE FUNERALS
AND A
DOG

VIRGINIA'S MEMORIAL SERVICE

Baxter is invited to Virginia's memorial service at San Diego Hospice and The Institute for Palliative Care. We are honored. The three of us enter, and Donna welcomes us. "Please sit up front. I am so glad that the three of you were able to make it. I am expecting you at the reception following this service."

I touch her arm. "Thank you for including us, for including Baxter."

"Baxter has to be here. He's the reason why you are here."

Before the service begins, Donna addresses those gathered. "Hello, everyone, thank you for being here today. Before we get started, I would like to introduce Baxter, Dennis, and Melissa, volunteers here at hospice. They have been very special for me and my mom. Baxter has brought us many memorable moments of joy and comfort. I will never forget him. He would visit us and get in my mom's bed; my bed, too. He made her smile, laugh, and recall special times in her life. He is a real gift."

At the reception, Baxter bonds with Emma, a friend of Donna's family. I'm not sure who is cuter, Emma or Baxter.

> "BAXTER HAS BROUGHT US MANY MEMORABLE MOMENTS OF JOY AND COMFORT. HE MADE MY MOM SMILE, LAUGH, AND RECALL SPECIAL TIMES IN HER LIFE. HE IS A REAL GIFT."

JESSE'S FUNERAL

Many of Jesse's family members already know Baxter. Several have met him at hospice, and others have been given a vivid description of his wondrous ways. Many people walk up to him to say hello and thank him for helping Jesse and Emma, Jesse's mother.

At the reception following the funeral, Baxter meets Indy, who made a special blanket

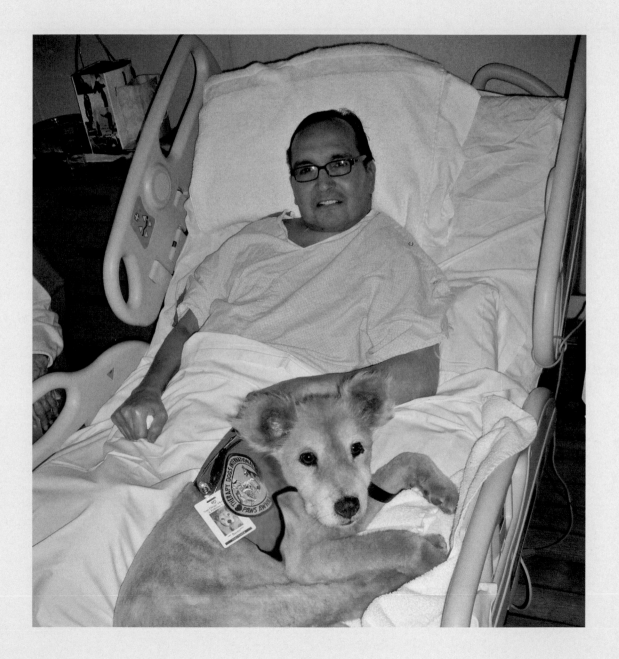

for Emma to give to him. Indy sits by Baxter throughout the entire reception and says, "Baxter, I now understand why Jesse and Emma fell in love with you."

CORAZÓN'S FUNERAL

The Aguilars ask us to come to Corazón's funeral and reception.

Baxter is his usual perfect self as we enter the church. He sits on his bed in the rear of the sanctuary, silent and still throughout the lengthy service.

Dennis and I wipe away our tears as we listen to the raw beauty of what each family member says. When Gina, the final family member, speaks, we are again reminded of the magnitude of what Baxter does as a certified therapy dog. "We want to thank Baxter for what he did for our family, for my mother, for all of us."

More tears. Several people in the back pew figure out just why Baxter is here and start whispering and pointing. I am so proud of Baxter. I reach for Dennis's hand, and we leave for the burial site.

We have reaffirmed that our experiences with Baxter are the most touching moments of our lives.

WE HAVE REAFFIRMED THAT OUR EXPERIENCES WITH BAXTER ARE THE MOST TOUCHING MOMENTS OF OUR LIVES.

BAXTER'S
RÉSUMÉ

MS. JAN CETTI
SAN DIEGO HOSPICE AND
THE INSTITUTE FOR PALLIATIVE MEDICINE

Dear Ms. Cetti,

My mother, Jeanne St. Mar, was blessed with spending her final days at San Diego Hospice and The Institute for Palliative Medicine this spring. (She made her transition on Easter.) After months at the V.A. hospital and two difficult weeks caring for her at home, we thought we had gone to heaven when we brought her to the in-patient facility.

One of the special staff members that touched my mom's and our lives was the angel/dog Baxter. My mom was deeply affected by her interaction with Baxter. I noticed how relaxed she became when he was with her—looking into her eyes as if she were his lifelong companion. She didn't feel like she had to "entertain" or stand on ceremony, which she always did with people. I heard her give some nice "sighs" as she stroked him. I think, too, that she felt that she was comforting Baxter, after hearing of his abusive early years.

How special for her to have a feeling of giving to someone, since throughout her illness she was concerned that she could no longer be helpful. She would talk about what Baxter's life must've been like, with a concerned look on her face. She was able to be mothering towards Baxter, whereas with her kids the roles had been reversed for sometime.

Baxter in particular and pet therapy in general makes use of the healing power of touch. In Baxter's case you just want to touch and hug him! He is so receptive and gentle. (Baxter is the most relaxed dog I've seen.) He is perfect for the quiet, gentle hospice environment, and wasn't at all perturbed with us all wanting to touch him. Our family (from my mom's only grandson, to her kids, to her sister and nieces and nephew) still talks about Baxter! My cousin, who is a veterinarian, tells his friends that Baxter is unlike any other dog he's ever seen. We all agree. We all loved his peaceful, soulful presence. Baxter gave us a sweet, loving memory during a very sad time.

I'd like to thank you for the work you and San Diego Hospice are doing in setting a standard for the way we care for people at the end of life.

Sincerely,
Marilyn Muerth
(Daughter of Jeanne St. Mar)

SEPTEMBER 2, 2007
MS. JAN CETTI, PRESIDENT
SAN DIEGO HOSPICE AND
THE INSTITUTE FOR PALLIATIVE MEDICINE

Dear Ms. Cetti,

In April of this year, our loved one, Jesse Lara, was admitted to the ICC at San Diego Hospice.

We felt from the minute we walked through your doors that the calm and peaceful environment was exactly where Jesse needed to be. The five weeks of loving care that followed at San Diego Hospice were far beyond any expectations we could have had.

Words cannot express our appreciation for the kind, attentive, and supportive care provided to Jesse and our family by the entire staff at the ICC.

There is one particular angel that truly touched our lives at San Diego Hospice. The day that Baxter, the therapy dog, entered Jesse's room was like a gift from above. He made an immediate connection with Jesse—gently snuggling up to him on the bed. His sweet, loving, and compassionate disposition brought joy and love into the room each and every visit. Whoever thought, at a time of such sorrow and pain, that you could actually fall in love again? And fall in love we did—the entire family—with this canine angel named Baxter.

Baxter's visits gave us something to look forward to, something new to love and care about, newfound happiness and incredible comfort.

The story of our touching experience proves how giving both humans and animals can be. Our family now firmly believes that reaching out and helping each other goes beyond faith, color, and even species.

God bless you all,
Emma Lara and Family

August 28, 2007
Jan Cetti, President and CEO
San Diego Hospice and
The Institute for Palliative Medicine

Dear President Cetti,

My dear mother, Virginia Smith, received hospice care in the latter part of 2006, and passed on December 15. She was amazed and so very grateful for the personal and compassionate care your organization offered her. She was the type of person everyone loved. During her last days, she received several visits from Dennis and Melissa Bussey with Baxter, the therapy dog. That was truly the high point of her stay at hospice.

Dennis and Melissa came in one day and asked if they could bring Baxter in to lay with mom. She was too weak to move much, so they placed him on the bed with her. My mom stroked Baxter as he lay on her bed, comforting her in a way no human can. She had been a dog lover all her life and missed having her little dog there with her. Melissa talked to my mom, entertained her, and made her laugh. She has a wonderful sense of humor—great medicine for the ailing! Dennis provides comfort and support with his quiet compassion. They make quite a trio. We were all so touched by this team, we took a video of their second visit (about a half hour long). They offered to come back again and again, spending their own time to provide comfort not only to my mom but also to me. We were very close and it was hard for me to face the fact I was losing her. I remember one time lying on the floor, hugging Baxter. He looked at me with wise understanding eyes and let me cry—really an amazing dog. It's wonderful to know there are people in the word like the Busseys and dogs like Baxter.

Sincerely,
Donna Carr

HOSPICE
STAFF

Caring for those who are facing the ends of their lives is one of the most challenging jobs we can imagine. During our years volunteering, we have been amazed again and again by the compassion and respect that the staff members of San Diego Hospice and The Institute for Palliative Medicine show to the patients and their families and friends. They truly embrace the hospice mission: "No one should die alone; no one should die in pain." We are so honored that they have allowed Baxter, Dennis, and me to be part of this mission.

DR. DORIS HOWELL

GLORIA JERNIGAN
CNA

JOAN COONEY
FOOD SERVICE

ANG HO LY
HOUSEKEEPING

JOYCE LA RUE
RN

DR. PAMELA CLOSE

MICHELLE SILVA
ACUPUNCTURE/MASSAGE

DR. PETER STEFANIDES

HOLLY DAVLIN
SOCIAL WORKER

MICHELLE LESCAULT
RN

KAREN ALIOTO RN
& BARBARA HESS RN

SARAH WHITE
CNA

ARTURO HERNANDEZ
CUSTODIAN

BARBARA STRAWN
CNA

CHAPLAIN
MAUREEN KELLY

JAN KAPCHINSKE
RN

TINA SOURIAL
RN

AMY STEFFEN
UNIT CLERK

DR. HOLLY YANG

SHARON MARHEINE
CNA

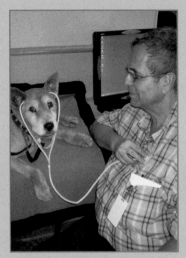

ROGER STRONG
NP

CHARITO MILLER
RN

DAN BJIERKE
COUNSELOR

DORANNE GODWIN
PATIENT CARE VOLUNTEER

GIGI RAYGOR
RN

RODNEY SCHWAN
AROMATHERAPIST

PAULA ENGEL
RN

RACHEL ESQUIBEL
CNA

CHAPLAIN
LISA MCCULLOUGH

DR. SHANNON MOORE

DR. CINDY TORAYA

YOU —— AND YOUR —— THERAPY DOG

Many of you, I suppose, believe unequivocally that your dog, right now, will make the best therapy dog on the planet. And perhaps this is true. It's not, though, just about your dog, or your dog's spirit. It's about you and your spirit, too. The two of you must have a relationship where you work as a team to serve others, to bring comfort to others, and to assuage pain, both emotional and physical.

Let me tell you what you want to look for in yourself and your dog to be considered as a winning therapy team.

It starts with this powerful, incredible urge to share your dog with others. You see something angelic in your dog: a bountiful love coupled with a pervasive sweetness that is life-transforming for you, and that, you believe, will be for other individuals as well. You recognize that you have a dog who connects with people, who's sensitive and perceptive.

You must also have the ability to engender self-esteem in your dog. You want your dog to be confident in strange or unfamiliar places, and to like strange and unfamiliar people. Much of this I accomplished by taking Baxter to an array of diverse environments where he socialized with all kinds of people.

"Wow," you might say, "my dog already has all these qualifications." That's great. Do you also have these characteristics? You see, you are the core of your dog's training. It is your personality that will demonstrate this confidence in your dog. Like your children, your dog will mirror you.

Remember, it's all about love, comfort, and service. You and your dog are there to give moments of love, to provide comfort, and to offer service to the patients, families, and friends.

Several years ago, Dennis, Baxter, and I were visiting a patient at San Diego Hospice and The Institute for Palliative Medicine. A family member observed Baxter interacting with her aunt. Before she left, she introduced herself: "I'm Aleita Downer and I train therapy dogs. I must tell you that your dog is the most amazing therapy dog that I've ever seen."

Aleita has a company, Cape-Able Canines, that has been in business in San Diego for twenty years. It wouldn't be an exaggeration to say that she is an authority on therapy dogs. I recently contacted Aleita and asked her to elaborate on why Baxter is the perfect therapy dog.

"Oh, sure, I remember Baxter," she said. "How could I forget him? It's been over two years, but I clearly remember him. He's unique because he's so old, yet so willing. Nothing has to be done his way. He's still willing to let people handle him. Most dogs are repelled by the smell of death. Baxter seemed immune to that. He's exceptional to be so available at such an old age."

Aleita says there are about eight features of a good therapy dog:

- Attraction to people

- Willingness to be handled

- Patience

- Good socialization—a calm demeanor, an ability to withstand loud, clanging noises and wailing sounds, as well as to ride in the car without getting sick

- Flexibility

- Friendly nature

- Special desire to be around people

- The dog must be controllable, reliable, and predictable.

All of these qualifications are necessary in order for your dog to pass the certification test, which is administered by any one of four organizations: The Bright and the Beautiful Therapy Dogs, Inc.; Delta Society; Therapy Dogs, Inc.; and Therapy Dogs International, Inc., which certified Baxter. You can log on to any one of these organizations to find out more information.

Each year, you will renew your dog's certification by paying a minimal fee, which includes a liability policy required by most institutions where you and your dog will be volunteering. The main reason for the test is to ensure that nothing will incite your dog to be aggressive.

This experience, if you and your dog pass the test, will change your life, as well as your relationship with your dog, forever. You will savor the moments, cherish the love of your dog, and triumph in making a difference, one moment at a time, in someone else's life.

THIS OLD
DOG
OF MINE

Baxter is now eighteen years old as of March 23, 2008. When he turns twenty, I plan on having a big celebration to honor his service over the years, as well as his gift of endless love. I'm tempting him with this party in hope that he will want to reach that age for me . . . for him . . . and for all whose lives he has touched and will touch over the remainder of his life. I want him to live forever, because he brings that much joy to my life . . . every day . . . every moment.

Not unlike humans, older dogs need a job, a mission. They need a place to go, something to do, or they will sleep more than they will live. Stimulating your dog is one way to keep him alive longer. I am sure that Baxter's job as a certified therapy dog has provided him with more love and demanded more from him in his later years.

How old is old when it comes to a dog? It all depends. Size, breed, pedigree or mix, and the dog's overall health all matter. Baxter, a love breed, reached the venerable age of eighteen because I am forever mindful of signs that indicate he needs medical attention. He receives the best veterinary care available. And, when he turned twelve, his veterinarian, Dr. Karen Hackett, recommended that he have a senior blood panel twice a year.

After this, the most essential ingredient for his care is exercise. On many days he's like a stubborn old man who hurts and doesn't want to do the walky-walky thing (which now is more the shuffle-shuffle). Every morning and every evening, we shuffle. It can take as long as fifteen minutes for Baxter to get started. He'll stop-start, stop-start, and I will try several techniques to get him going. I'll pick him up and take him to the opposite side of the street, I'll get down on the sidewalk and hold him and tell him how much I love him, or I'll even get involved in a standoff until he moves. And if none of this works, I'll put him in the car, drive one mile, and start the walk from that spot. But I never give in to him unless I truly believe he's incapable of walking. Invariably, he will walk twice a day, an hour each time, and he always seems happier after a walk. I do give him a treat when we get home, which is only a handful of his prescription food. I always give Baxter his dog food—and nothing else.

Baxter stays groomed. I am his groomer, which allows me to constantly inspect him. I clean his ears, brush his teeth, comb his tail, and condition his fur several times a week. I check his foot pads and at night put bag balm on the ones that are splitting. I massage Baxter and give him lots and lots of kisses, hugs, pats, and strokes.

And, lastly, I talk to him . . . a lot. I snuggle with him before he goes to bed and tuck him in under a baby blanket. I make sure that he's neither too hot nor too cold. He wears a cooling jacket in the summer months , which seems to help, especially with going back and forth to work. A wet towel draped over his body works just as well.

I never ask him to lie on the pavement. I have a travel dog bed that unrolls, which I take with us everywhere, or I put him in his red padded wagon.

s frail, underweight, and very slow. I coddle him, keep cushy things
r him, and move at his pace. I pick him up when he falls and brush
e keeps going on his own volition, as if nothing out of the ordinary
ccepts his frailties.

now when life is too much for him. He barks for help, pants for
s awake when he's in pain. When all this gets to be too much, I
ill communicate that he's ready to say good-bye forever.

HOW BAXTER COMMUNICATES

In the last year or so, Baxter's health has become visibly more f
stance quite wobbly. He now weighs only 35 pounds, down from
splotchy and in places there are cinnamon colored tufts coming fr
black pigment. His intelligent bump protrudes even more and it lool
Mohawk growing from its surface. He is like the Velveteen Rabbit, lo
ately that every part of him is tattered and frayed except for his heart, which remains
whole and full of love. His skin has random dark spots as if he had too much sun
and too little sun block. Still, Baxie is loveable, huggable, and irresistible.

His gait is more and more compromised. When he shuffles along, he moves as if
he has his first pair of high heels on his back paws, which now, like the front ones,
look like mittens. He often falls and cannot get himself back up. To communicate
this, he barks until I arrive to pick him up and re-start him back on his way.

Before, Baxter rarely barked. Now it is routine for him to apprise me of where
he is and what he needs. He's not shy for words; on the contrary, his barks come
out loud and clear. There are neither tears nor whimpers when he needs assistance.
Only a soft, deep-throated bark that says it all. Baxter doesn't bark at people, other
dogs, or things. He only barks to communicate that he needs something from me.

With Baxter, I don't really need to know what time it is. He barks to let me
know. He barks for breakfast, he barks for lunch, and he barks for dinner. He even
barks for snacks, which consist of the same prescription dog food that I give him
at meals. If I forget his medications, he barks until I put all eight pills in some
prescription wet food and place them in his mouth. Baxter does love to eat, but
I know he lives to love.

When it's his bedtime, 9 P.M., he barks. He'll either go to my bedroom and stand there and bark or come get me and start barking. He will do this until I go to bed with him. He can no longer negotiate the doggie door; hence, he barks each time he needs to go to the bathroom.

My hope is that he will communicate to me when it's time for the end of his life. That moment will be anguishing to decipher, but I owe it to him to answer his request. For now, though, I will continue to love him moment to moment and cherish him with all my heart.

THERAPY DOG TEAM TRAINING

By J. Aleita Downer,
OWNER OF CAPE-ABLE CANINES

The Cape-Able Canines Therapy Dog Team Training workshop grew out of my own experiences when I began doing therapy dog work. My dog Summer and I were evaluated, photographed, health tested, and "oriented," but we were never trained to do the actual work of therapy visits. Some humorous . . . and not so humorous events happened as a result of this lack of training. We created a six-week workshop that meets for two hours a week to answer handlers' questions and teach the handlers and dogs the specialty commands and positioning. We discuss "icebreakers" and pacing, safety, and reasons to cancel a visit. Students learn public–sensitive correction and canine management techniques.

Ideally, there are three members to the therapy team: the handler, the dog, of course, and an escort. All three benefit from preparation and training for this important work.

THE HANDLER

The handler's job is to focus attention on the client or patient, while still monitoring the dog's activities, behavior, and stress level. That takes practice! The therapy dog handler does much of the work behind the scenes; he has an obligation to see that the dog is clean, well groomed, parasite free, quiet, and well behaved when in public. If a dog is going to live, work, and socialize in a human world, he must observe a higher standard of behavior than a pet dog. The handler's job is to insure that his dog does not do anything considered inappropriate by human standards and that he is never an inconvenience to the public in any way.

The handler is usually also the trainer, which is desirable. During the training process the dog and handler are also bonding, establishing good communication and a strong working relationship.

THE DOG

There cannot be too much training for therapy work. In addition to knowing many commands, a therapy dog must be under control, easy to walk, have great social skills, and be able to pay attention under very distracting circumstances. That's a tall order!

Training is the key: I usually recommend dogs and their handlers attend a minimum of a six-week puppy class, followed by general obedience series and level II training. Trick training also comes in handy for visits where entertaining is your goal, or when the patient prefers not to touch your dog.

Socialization, or exposure to a large variety of enrichment activities, should begin early and be ongoing! It can be time consuming to socialize your puppy or dog, but hospital visits can include many surprises and a therapy dog needs to have confidence, resilience, and a high level of trust in his handler's ability to be a strong leader. This can be accomplished by exposing your dog to as many sights, sounds, and smells as possible. While all dogs benefit from socialization, these socialization exercises are crucial to a therapy dog's success.

THE ESCORT

The escort's job is to organize and facilitate the therapy visit by picking up any needed supplies at the volunteer office, taking blank visitation sheets to the charge nurses on each floor, and getting permission to see patients who make special requests for visits. The escort also helps by introducing the dog and handler to the patient, taking photos to leave with the patient, and assisting with the flow of the visit itself.

The escort plays another important role. In case of an incident, he serves the hospital, the patient, and the handler as an extra pair of eyes and ears!

TESTING AND CERTIFICATION

Not everyone or every dog that wants to be involved with pet therapy is appropriate. Volunteers must apply to programs and earn the opportunity to participate by meeting entrance requirements. Safety is the overriding concern in determining which dogs are appropriate for therapy programs and which are not. Dogs are screened for good health, appropriate temperament, and obedience. Volunteers are evaluated for adequate handling skills. These must go together.

There are lots of tests that can help determine whether your dog is right for, and prepared to do, therapy dog work. Most therapy dog programs require that dogs pass the American Kennel Club's Canine Good Citizen Test. The CGC tests good manners, not precision training, and the dog must succeed in all ten parts in order to pass the test.

Each program also devises and administers a certification test of their own to determine your dog's friendliness and level of training.

Some therapy dog programs also require a passing grade on the American Temperament Test. As the name implies, the ATT evaluates breeding, not training. The test is designed to measure personality traits like aggressiveness or shyness, stability, sociability, and instinct to protect self and master. It simulates everyday social situations, which are both friendly and threatening, so that the tester can measure the appropriateness of the dog's reactions.

IS THERAPY WORK
RIGHT FOR MY DOG AND FOR ME?

In general, a therapy dog needs to be even-tempered and good-natured, friendly and curious, well socialized and able to work with a variety of people. Slippery floors, stairs, or loud noises should not bother her. He should be secure with the handler's leadership, and okay with being poked, prodded, and hugged, and trained well enough to show good manners around food trays and bedpans!

The ideal therapy dog handler is a warm, caring, responsible person who is disability-aware and enjoys social interaction. It is important that the human partner in this team is able to take care of herself emotionally, as working with the clientele that we do—hospital patients, the elderly, the incarcerated or the neglected—can be upsetting. There is a definite time commitment involved for training and grooming, as well as for visits.

How do I find a trainer?

Finding a dog trainer is easy! Finding a GOOD trainer is a little bit harder. Finding a trainer with therapy dog experience is tricky.

- Ask questions: Interview your potential trainer by phone or email. Find out if they have therapy dog classes and work experience.

- Check references: Ask for the names of previous and present students and contact them.

- Ask for and verify credentials: No state credentials are required of a dog trainer, but most experienced trainers will have trade affiliations, awards, or training certificates.

What organizations
train and credential dogs?

There are significant benefits to joining an existing, organized, recognized therapy dog organization. A quick search of the internet will help you locate one in your area. In addition to the all-important liability insurance, you may receive an evaluation of your dog's suitability for therapy dog work, training for you and your dog, information concerning disabilities and medical issues important to therapy dog work, and a network of friends with similar interests. You will not have to address problem situations by yourself. You will have colleagues with whom to exchange advice and information. Many organizations perform group visits at facilities, which can provide fun and variety. Many offer a newsletter and other useful publications; if the organizations are charitable, contributions and dues may be tax-deductible. Many also schedule visits and facilities for you. Membership in an organization lends you credibility and helps to support a standard of performance for therapy dogs and handlers everywhere.

Various therapy dog organizations offer a range of services; some are targeted at the independent handler, whereas some provide more structure and organization. The key is selecting a program that fits your preferences and style. Think about the level of service and involvement that you want from your organization. Therapy dog work should be fun and satisfying; choose an organization that helps you meet your goals and that takes away some of the stress and uncertainty so that you can have a good time.

SUMMER LOVE: A SUCCESS STORY

When our therapy dog team, my golden retriever Summer, my escort, and I, entered the pediatric intensive care unit, one of the nurses snapped, "Get that dog out of here."

I was startled and a little hurt. Another nurse rushed us toward the door. "This isn't the time for you to be here. This little girl is just beginning to rouse out from her coma, and we can't seem to keep her here," she explained.

Just as the door swished shut on the hectic scene, the nurse at the foot of the bed jumped up. "Wait a minute, this may be just what we're looking for!" He ran into the hall and ushered us back into the room, asking if I could get Summer-Dog to do exactly what he told me she should do. I said, "Of course I can," as my stomach took a little lurch.

I remembered every mistake from the past, like the time I issued the command "jump on" instead of "paws up" and Summer landed, uninvited, in the middle of the patient's bed. The elderly patient reassured me by saying, "That's okay, honey . . . that's the leg they amputated."

When the crowd around the bed parted to make way for us, we saw a little girl, perhaps 12 years old, who appeared to be deeply asleep. My confidence slipped a little further as confusion reigned.

"Have the dog jump on the bed."

"No, she might be afraid of dogs!"

"Bring the dog to the end of the bed so she'll see it if she wakes."

"Can you make the dog bark or something?"

As a therapy dog handler, my first responsibility is always the well-being of my dog. Summer was beginning to mirror the feelings in the room and showed signs of frustration and stress. I wanted to be helpful, but I knew if the situation got worse, we would have to leave. I asked if my escort could bring a chair near the bed, and for permission to have Summer jump onto it. I suggested she be allowed to work from that position.

Suddenly, everything fell into place. The nurse nearest Summer took the little girl's hand in hers and stroked Summer's head with it. A nurse at the end of the bed tapped and tickled the girl's feet. The girl's mother cried softly as she stroked her daughter's hair and called her name.

Our eyes were fixed to the girl's face as we watched for a flicker of an eyelid or a movement of her head. One by one, the nurses abandoned their efforts, murmuring comforting words about "a gradual process," "a good sign," "maybe next time."

Reluctant to give up, we all lingered just a minute longer. Then, we saw a single tear roll down the little girl's cheek. Her hand opened and closed, grasping Summer's fur.

As a therapy dog handler, I spend hours before every visit grooming my dog, exercising her, preparing costumes and "props," reviewing old commands, and teaching new ones.

Often the hospital visit is emotionally and physically tiring for us both. Sometimes the hospital staff seems tired, overworked, uncooperative, or unappreciative. Occasionally, you find an empty bed when you step into your favorite patient's room.

But, sometimes you get to see the bright blue eyes and pretty smile of a little girl who has been in a coma. And then it's all worthwhile.

Published by Sage Press
P.O. Box 500341 • San Diego, CA 92150-0341 • 858.676.5359
orders@MomentswithBaxter.com • www.MomentswithBaxter.com

Produced by BookStudio, LLC
www.bookstudiobooks.com

Edited by Karla Olson, BookStudio, LLC
Copy editing by Lisa Wolff
Book Design by Charles McStravick, Artichoke Design

ANGEL
Copyright 1997 Sony/ATV Songs LLC, Tyde Music. All rights administered by
Sony/ATV Music Publishing, 8 Music Square West, Nashville, TN 37203.

Printed by Everbest Printing Company Ltd., China

ISBN 13: 978-0-9818813-0-0
ISBN 10: 0-9818813-0-0

Publisher's Cataloging-in-Publication Data

Joseph, Melissa.

Moments with Baxter / Melissa Joseph. -- San Diego, CA : Sage
Press, c2009.

p. ; cm.

ISBN: 978-0-9818813-0-0

1. Dogs--Therapeutic use--Biography. 2. Service dogs--
Biography. 3. Hospice care. 4. Human-animal relationships. I. Title.

RM931.D63 J67 2009   2008933589
636.7/0886--dc22   0904